Black Income in India

Black Income in India

SURAJ B. GUPTA

Sage Publications
NEW DELHI/NEWBURY PARK/LONDON

For dear Mansi and Utkersh

First published in 1992 by

Sage Publications India Pvt Ltd
M-32 Greater Kailash Market-I
New Delhi 110 048

Sage Publications Inc
2455 Teller Road
Newbury Park, California 91320

Sage Publications Ltd
6 Bonhill Street
London EC2A 4PU

Published by Tejeshwar Singh for Sage Publications India Pvt Ltd., phototypeset by Pagewell Phototypesetters, Pondicherry, and printed at Chaman Enterprises, Delhi.

Library of Congress Cataloging-in-Publication Data

Gupta, Suraj B.
Black income in India / Suraj B. Gupta.
p. cm.
Includes bibliographical references and index.
1. Tax evasion—India. 2. Income tax—India. 3. Excise tax—India. 4. Smuggling—India. 5. Informal sector (Economics)—Taxation—India. I. Title.
HJ4766.Z7E754 1992 364.1′33′0954—dc20 92–32148

ISBN: 0–8039–9453–2 (US-cloth) 0–8039–9454–0 (US-paper)
81–7036–311–X (India-cloth) 81–7036–312–8 (India-paper)

Contents

List of Tables

Preface

Black income comprises a very significant and fast growing element of India's economy. It has already afflicted most walks of life and economic activities. Yet, it has not attracted enough attention from scholars. This volume examines this hydra-headed problem in its full diversity and various manifestations. Unlike other studies, it does not restrict itself to an examination of the evasion of personal income tax only, but covers instead a much wider and varied territory, going from the evasion of excise and customs duties to smuggling. It provides rough estimates of black income, both in the aggregate and for individual sources, for three selected years of the 1980s. The consequences of black operations are very serious. They have been discussed under three interconnected heads—political, economic and social. This is followed by a brief policy review. One important feature of our discussion is the hypothesis that political-cum-bureaucratic corruption lies at the root of most black operations. This itself is determined by certain factors which are discussed in the book.

Overall, the book should serve as the basis for the formulation as well as the evaluation of policy measures designed to check black income. It should also go a long way to explain why a holistic approach is required to successfully control the menace of black income and that particularistic measures can have, at best, only limited success. Insofar as recent structural reforms are moving the economy towards a more liberal and market-friendly regime, reducing the degree of administrative regulation and control (through licensing) of the economy, the opportunities for political and bureaucratic corruption are likely to be reduced significantly. Yet, large-scale tax evasion, leakages from public expenditure, bribery and malpractices of several kinds have, over time, become so ingrained in the behaviour pattern of the public, politicians and government employees at all levels that sustained all-round efforts for substantial improvement in the mores of the public and the government apparatus are required to discourage black operations significantly.

Several colleagues and friends have helped me in various ways in writing this book. Particular mention needs to be made of Professors V.N. Pandit, K.L. Krishna, S.D. Tendulkar, K. Krishnamurty, Drs Pulin Nayak, B.L. Pandit and, most of all, Khan Masood Ahmad. My thanks to each one of them. The present format of the book owes much to the suggestions made by an anonymous reader of the first draft, to whom I am grateful. I would also like to thank Ms Primila Lewis for all her advice. I would like to acknowledge with thanks the service readily provided by the staff of the Ratan Tata Library (Delhi School of Economics). Finally, I would like to record my gratefulness to my wife, Manorama, for making my task of writing this book pleasant in every way.

Delhi SURAJ B. GUPTA
June 1992

1

Introduction

With the rapid growth of black economy in India and its attainment of a level high enough to be able to command a significantly large proportion of India's economy and influence greatly the working of its political system, it has become imperative to study the nature and functioning of the black economy. Black operations adversely affect the functioning of the economy and the political system and the various institutions related to them. The 'deviations' from the 'normal' so caused bring about further structural and functional changes in the overall political economy of a country and reduce it to a state of interminable sickness and morbidity. All policy measures, howsoever well-conceived, in such a state get variously miscarried and, hence, lose much of their efficacy. These generalised statements about a sick politico-economic system need to be thoroughly probed and substantiated as far as possible, the particular ailments or afflictions specifically identified and diagnosed, and the harm done by them to the system clearly analysed.

The black economy is said to have taken birth during the scarcity conditions of the Second World War when controls on the distribution and prices of goods in short supply (such as foodgrains and cloth) led to the emergence of black markets, and hoarding in them. Black market prices, which were higher than the controlled prices, gave birth to 'black incomes' (commonly called 'black money'). In other words, money received in such deals was not disclosed, and not entered into the books of account to avoid severe penalties. So, tax on such incomes got fully evaded. Besides, large amounts of unaccounted gains were also made by many from war-time supply and construction contracts, and so on.

The war-time baby of the black economy grew up fast and spread its tentacles far and wide throughout the economy. Unscruplous traders and supply contractors took full advantage of the Partition of India and the resulting influx of refugees and their relief and rehabilitation. Similarly, the spurt in economic activities under planning and successive five-year plans has created umpteen opportunities for sundry contractors, businessmen-racketeers, politicians and bureaucrats to make quick money, and a large part of it in black (or unaccounted). The grant of industrial and import licences, quotas and permits, transactions in urban real estate, smuggling, manipulation of import and export invoices, and so on, are some illustrative examples of the black-economy operations that have caused serious damage to the 'official' (or 'white') economy. All this has been accompanied by widespread bribery and corruption in practically all government services—from the police to the judiciary, and from village patwaris to senior executives and politicians of all hues.

Black income is now an all-pervasive phenomenon that requires the serious attention of social scientists. At least three aspects of this phenomenon deserve special attention.

First, in terms of its sources of generation and proximate determinants, black income is not one homogeneous category, but many. It is not limited only to the evasion of income tax, but extends to the evasion of all kinds of taxes and goes even beyond them in the form, for example, of bribes, smuggling and leakages from government expenditure. Therefore, the study of black-income generation by main areas of economic activity is essential for understanding the anatomy as well as the pathology of black operations and for designing, administering and evaluating effective policy measures to counter the menace of black income, black wealth and black operations. If black income is not purely (or even largely) due to the evasion of personal income tax, a policy designed only to plug this loophole is doomed to fail.

The forementioned observation has an important implication for the definition of black income. It is customary to define black income narrowly with respect to only income tax (personal) and say that it is that income which, though taxable, is not reported to the tax authorities and thereby income tax on it is evaded. But, since taxes are not of only one variety (such as, income tax) but of several varieties (for example, excise duties, customs duties and sales tax), and the evasion of each of them is rampant in the Indian economy, it is essential to broaden the definition of black income substantially to include all taxable but unreported income and the amount of taxes evaded on all excisable output, sales, imports, and so on. Further, black income also includes incomes which arise through leakages in government expenditure, bribery, smuggling and other unreportable activities.

Second, the many means of black-income generation deserve to be cross-classified under a few empirically meaningful categories to help analysis as well as suitable policy formulation. To begin with, the definition of black income clearly suggests a twofold classification of all black income into unreportable and reportable black incomes. Unreportable black income is income that cannot be reported for tax purposes, simply because the manner in which it is raised is illegitimate or illegal. Reportable black income, on the other hand, is income that is earned through legitimate means, but is concealed from the tax authorities. In this case, the sole objective is to evade taxes on it. This distinction suggests, in a simple manner, that not all black income is motivated solely by the objective of tax evasion and hence is not the function of taxes alone, unless we assert that the subset of unreportable black income constitutes a null set.

Unreportable Black Income

The forms and sources of unreportable black income are many. I shall compress them under the following four heads: crime income, bribe income, black-market income and black-wealth income.

Crime Income: Such income is derived through the use of criminal means, such as robbery, theft, drug trafficking, smuggling of contraband, trade in vice, sale of official secrets, spying, adulteration of food items, illicit distillation, counterfeiting and economic fraud.

Bribe Income: Such income is derived by persons in authority or their agents, whether in public or private employment, through the sale of favours to the briber.

Black-Market Income: Black marketing involves either black (higher than officially fixed) prices or black quantities or both. Black (market) prices have been a common phenomenon when commodities (for instance, steel and cement) have been subjected to price control. Black quantities are traded all the time in the economy—such as all smuggled goods, adulterated and spurious goods and quantities which have evaded excise duties on them. Any extra income derived from charging higher black prices or the income from the sale of black quantities, then, is black-market income and unreportable to the tax authorities.

Black-Wealth Income: Black wealth is held in various forms, such as real estate, jewellery, business assets, foreign currency accounts and cash and bank deposits. Owner-occupied property, jewellery and cash, and so on add only a flow of utility, not pecuniary income. Some wealth may also be held *benami* (fictitiously). Some other black wealth (especially business assets) may have been converted into white wealth through various devices. Yet, there may be some income from black wealth (as, for example, interest income from loans of black funds), which will not be declarable to tax authorities, as the source of this income itself is black. It is generally held that a very large and growing amount of black funds are circulating in the Indian economy.

Reportable Black Income

As already mentioned, reportable black income is income that is earned through legitimate economic activities or transactions, but becomes 'black' when it is suppressed and not reported to the tax authorities so as to evade taxes that will fall on it. Such income arises in more or less all income-earning activities where all income is not automatically recorded. Thus, all wage and salary income in organised employment, corporate dividends, interest and rental income from the organised sector borrowers and tenants and income from all payments received against proper receipts or documents are presumably always reported for tax purposes, unless otherwise exempted by tax laws. But a significant part of business income, and the income of self-employed professionals (such as film artists, medical practitioners, lawyers, architects, engineers and chartered accountants), and even labour income in unorganised activities, though earned legitimately, is suppressed in a wide variety of ways, some legal and some illegal. These almost always involve false maintenance of accounts, as some incomes are not shown at all or not in full in books of account and some expenditures are overreported. The opportunities for such underreporting of income and overreporting of expenses are several. (Underinvoicing of exports and overinvoicing of imports, especially when foreign exchange sells on premium, is alleged to be quite common.) Their exploitation is advised and even 'managed' by tax consultants, lawyers, accountants and other middlemen, and abetted by tax officials, other government functionaries, politicial elite and other wheeler-dealers of power against bribes in one form or other. These remarks are equally applicable to excisable output and taxable imports and sales where, again, tax evasion is practised on a large scale.

Third, it deserves to be noted that the black-income activity does not end with only generating black income, but that it results in black consumption and black saving, which when accumulated results in black wealth. Thus, black consumption, black saving and black wealth are essential correlates of black income and vitiate further the working of the economy, polity and society. On the basis of causal empiricism, it may be said that the bulk of black income accrues to the already rich and that, within the rich class, too, black income is highly unevenly distributed in favour of the very rich. With the help of these assumptions and standard macroeconomic theory about the relation between income and consumption (or saving), we may derive the following two hypotheses: that a higher proportion of aggregate black income gets saved than of white income (though the forms in which savings are held or wealth accumulated leave much to be desired from the social point of view; that a large part of black consumption comprises luxuries, that is, the consumption expenditure out of black income is incurred largely on luxuries, ostentatious consumption and the vulgar display of riches at social functions (such as weddings and other social gatherings and parties). This has promoted the production, import and smuggling of luxury items in demand by the rich, and 'distorted' greatly the pattern of production and imports (including smuggling) and the allocation of scarce national resources even under planning. On the opposite end, the poor half of the country's large population who do not have any recourse to black income do not earn enough even to meet the basic necessities of life (of food, clothing and shelter) of their families.

The foregoing discussion has important implications for analysis as well as policy formulation. First, the consumption of non-durables does not generally leave behind concrete evidence of black consumption, except at the time of such consumption. However, checking them directly creates a lot of problems and will be administratively unfeasible. Although organising an expenditure tax has been found to be problematic, an attempt to directly check consumption expenditure is out of the question. Second, the possession of consumer durables can be more easily tracked through searches. But establishing their 'blackness' has not been a successful enterprise for the authorities. Third, looking for evidence of black income in various forms of black wealth is already a less than half-starter, because a large part of black income gets consumed and only the remaining gets saved and accumulated into wealth. Therefore, a scheme like the bearer bonds' scheme completely bypasses black consumption. Any stricter check on only 'black assets' is sure to encourage greater black consumption; it may or may not discourage black income generation.

Black savings result in the accumulation of *black wealth*. But black savings are not the only source of black wealth. Even hitherto white wealth, when unreported or underreported for purposes of tax on wealth (such as wealth tax, gift tax and various municipal taxes on property), takes on the character of black wealth. Then, some black wealth, like black income, is also acquired in non-reportable ways by crime, bribes or the black market. Thus, a flourishing black market in real estate has come to exist in all urban areas. In private deals, it is no longer possible to buy property against white money in full, because the seller does not like to declare the true price at which he is selling the property and thereby invite all manner of tax payments. In such a circumstance, the buyer with white money (if such parties truly exist any longer) is forced either to convert his white wealth at least partly into black wealth or forego the opportunity to acquire property he otherwise was desirous of acquiring.

Black wealth itself is held in various forms—almost all those forms in which white wealth is held, whether in cash, fixed deposits with banks, other financial assets or tangible assets. This is where and how *black money per se* appears on the scene. Black money, correctly speaking, is that part of black wealth which is held in the form of money (currency plus demand deposit of banks). In the context of the widespread misuse of the term 'black money,' it is important that the correct meaning of the term is firmly grasped, for the flagrant misuse of the term has been a potent source of confusion in the minds of not only the lay public, but also educated persons, even economists, and policy-makers and oftentimes has led to wrong analysis as well as policy prescriptions. Let me explain the point more concretely.

In common parlance, the term 'black money' is used, and quite generally so, for what we have called 'black income'. To an economist, such a misuse of the term is inexcusable on several counts. First, it involves stock-flow confusion, because whereas black money is a stock, black income is a flow. The stock-flow distinction is not of purely pedagogic importance, but of much practical significance, too. For the problem of black 'money' (income) is not purely one of unearthing stocks of black wealth (shortened to money), but equally or perhaps more importantly of curtailing substantially the continual fresh generation of black income flows. Thus understood, the simple-mindedness, if not the utter naivety, of such anti-black money (income) measures as the demonetisation of high denomination currency notes, or the issue of low-interest bearer bonds in exchange for 'black money,' becomes easily clear. Alternatively, such measures could be inspired by the pressures of black wealth holders for certain legal ways of converting black into white wealth and also misguiding the public about the sincerity of the government to curb black operations.

Second, a direct recognition of the more important problem of 'black income' leads naturally to the phenomenon of 'black consumption' (discussed earlier), which otherwise tends to get neglected.

Third, a consideration of 'black income,' instead of black money, leads equally naturally to the problem of black saving and black wealth and the several forms in which the two are held. So viewed, black money *per se* will automatically be seen as only a small part of black wealth. To the extent it (black money) is a major consideration for owners of black wealth to conceal it as well as they can, the allocation of black savings and the construction of private asset portfolios have generally tended to harm social interest. No doubt, a part of black savings (by firms) is continually reinvested in business, including inventory build-up of goods in short supply; another part of black household savings goes into socially unproductive assets, such as jewellery, urban land and luxury housing. A large part of black savings not invested in physical assets does not reach financial institutions (like banks, UTI and LIC,) or the organised capital market *via* corporate securities for fear of detection by the tax authorities. Much of it is assumed to flow into 'parallel' or unregulated credit markets. The size, *modus operandi* and functionaries of these markets are not fully known. But the usual broad guess is that the total number of borrowers, lenders and middlemen (finance brokers) in these markets is quite large; though the size of most individual loans given and taken may not be very large, the total amount of unregulated credit adds up to big amount which is growing all the time. The market in 'black credit' is, by any reckoning, a sizeable part of the unregualted credit market.

The true significance of black money is not to be measured by the proportion of black wealth it presumably represents. For, this may be quite small. A considerable portion of productive physical assets, real estate, jewellery and consumer durables have possibly been accumulated through black incomes and constitute big chunks of black wealth. Such an assertion cannot be supported by hard empirical evidence. But, given the tax structure that has existed in the economy since the early 1950s, such a judgement is inescapable.

The true role of black money *per se* is to facilitate 'black transactions' of all sorts, whether pertaining to the current production of goods and services, acquisition of existing assets, borrowing and lending or bribing as a medium of exchange. Not all black transactions need to involve only black money. Thus, sometimes white money is also paid for the acquisition of goods in the black market or as a bribe to public officials for various favours.

We cannot track down black income and black wealth via the intermediation of black money—in fact, black money is no more than a red herring. In order to check the problem of black economy, a well-thought out and well-coordinated frontal attack needs to be made on all the sources of black income which produce it all the time. For this, a careful examination of each of the main sources of black income, the methods used and factors responsible in each case is an essential precondition.

But such a task has not been attempted so far, as the mainstream economic theory bypasses all black-income phenomena. It is based on a false picture of ground reality. It presumes a world inhabited by 'honest' people—people who conduct their affairs according to the generally-accepted 'rules of the game'. In such a world, cases of fraud might not be fully absent, but such a world is presumed to be free from 'black operations' on an extensive scale, such as widely-practised evasion of taxes of all kinds, large-scale manipulation of accounts, large leakages of foreign exchange, heavy smuggling, bribing of officials, political corruption and self-serving by politicians and bureaucrats. The problem, then, is not one of mishandling these bitter facts of life, but one of ignoring them altogether, as if they do not take place in actual life or are not of large enough magnitude to merit the attention of high-bred economists. Pleas that economists should not be disturbed from their inbred pursuits, which have caused such a great implosion of issues on the road to scientific perfection of the subject of economics, are socially untenable.

The truth of the matter is that traditional economic theory at present does not possess a method of analysis whereby it can handle such a hot issue as black income. The problem can, however, be analysed in an extended framework of the political economy. I have not spelled out such a framework, as this lies outside the scope of this study. Coming back to the point under discussion, I stress that traditional economic theory neither takes cognizance of the ground reality of black operations nor possesses a paradigm within which to analyse them. The two shortcomings reinforce each other—the absence of a paradigm renders this part of reality irrelevant for the traditional economic theorist; the study of reality alone without a paradigm makes the whole output purely descriptive, which economist *qua* economist has taught himself to shun.

However, shunning of reality for too long has not been the tradition of economic theory. On the contrary, it has made important advances by recognising new developments in economic life and by forging new theories which attempt to explain these new developments. For example, there was a time when perfect competition was practically the only market structure studied and analysed, when this was also the dominant reality on the ground under early capitalism. But, with the growth of capitalism, new market forms generated by the growth of oligopolies and monopolies and multinational mega corporations have come to the fore.

With these developments, economic theory has also grown to capture and explain the new realities.

Domestically, monopoly capital exerts immense influence over all the levers of economic and political power. Internationally, big multinationals effectively rule small and weak nations and are able to exert a lot of pressure on the political economy of countries where these multinationals command a significant presence. In both kinds of cases, monopoly capital operates mainly through the market—the source of its political leverage and power is the economic power it holds. In the case of black operations, the roles of economic power and political power are practically reversed: here the power of the state is used as an instrument to derive black incomes through the violation of state laws and to get away with such violations almost with impunity through protection extended by someone connected (directly or indirectly) with the exercise of state power. This requires that the interaction between the economy and the state (and politics) be carefully studied, for which task the political economy approach is best suited. Also, the unstated but maintained assumption of honesty on the part of individual actors needs to be examined. We must also ask what happens when that motive force of economic action, self-interest (the bedrock of economic theory), jumps the rail of honesty. Are black operations a consequence or not? Similarly, we must also reckon with situations when the sentinels of law and order themselves break or evade law or become purchasable by bribers. Most of us face such unnerving questions in actual life. They point unmistakably towards the widespread presence of politico-administrative corruption at the root of most black operations in India. This will be discussed in the next chapter.

2

Political Corruption and Black Income

Introduction

We do not have a general theory of black income. In the past, limited attempts have been made to 'explain' income tax evasion in terms of the probability of detection and the punishment involved, given the tax laws of a country (for instance, see Srinivasan, 1973). But, income tax evasion is only one of the sources of black income, and that, too, not the most important, as the discussion in the next three chapters will show. Also, the discussion of tax evasion by economists tends to emphasise only the evader's behaviour and ignores the macro factors that govern the socio-political environs in which individual evaders (and other 'black operators') operate. In my view, such a macro environ prevailing in an economy is much more important than the individual propensity to evade a tax like income tax. The most outstanding feature of this macro environ in independent India has been evergrowing politico-administrative corruption. This corruption has both encouraged as well as abetted 'black operations' (black-income and -wealth) activities of all kinds, including criminal activities. Hence, we hypothesise that 'political corruption' defined broadly to include administrative corruption is the *sine qua non* of black economy. In turn, black-income activities need the patronage as well as protection of political leaders and administrators, gained through suitable bribes or considerations.

In the rest of this chapter, I shall first discuss the meaning and scope of political corruption and thereafter its main determinants.

Meaning and Scope of Political Corruption

Political corruption relates to political practices, acts, or decisions (or inducements to them), which involve departures from political norms or the proper conduct of political affairs and the proper use of political authority with a view to gain illegitimate advantage for the self or for favoured ones. I am using the word 'political' here broadly to include the activities of all the organs or apparatuses of the state and of the political parties. The advantages claimed are usually in the form of pay-offs (or bribes) in cash (at times in foreign currency or foreign bank accounts) or in kind, or counter-favours (actual or promised) to reliable intermediates, relatives, friends, or political supporters. They are gained in exchange for the disbursal of government favours bestowed on the payers of graft.

The favours take numerous forms, such as the preferential allotment of government contracts for supplies and construction of projects (which may run into billions of rupees), licenses, permits and quotas, protection or intervention against prosecution for diverse economic and even other serious offences committed, such as tax evasion, smuggling, black marketing, flouting of government rules and regulations (for instance, installation of unauthorised industrial capacity, unauthorised occupation of land or the construction of real estate, and evasion of land ceilings), falsification of information to gain undeserved allocation of institutional credit, foreign exchange and goods in short supply, subsidies, tax exemptions and other benefits. These are only illustrative examples. A complete listing of the forms favours exchanged take is neither feasible (as they are so many) nor necessary for our purpose.

Political corruption is such an important matter because, in today's age, politics has come to affect most spheres of social and economic life, and politics is now treated as another name of corruption. Politics now claims to operate as the society's major means of self-correction and development. Politicians, in their populist rhetoric and reformist zeal, now claim to act as the new messiahs of social salvation who want to rid society of all its ills.

Thereby, they have gained the apex of a new social hierarchy, which surpasses all other hierarchies. The ruling political leaders are treated with such awe and a vulgar display of sycophancy as was reserved for kings in earlier monarchical periods. It is now widely held that a large part of the Indian economy's malaise is due to the malfunctioning of India's political system and the rampant political corruption it nurses and harbours. Therefore, it is imperative to study political corruption in order to gain a deeper insight into this malady.

Political corruption in India has grown enormously. It acts like a giant octopus, spreading its tentacles far and wide, holding larger and larger areas of political and economic life in its vicious blood-sucking grip. It has become so all-pervasive and common that people have come to accept it as a part of life, as something normal. In private, this has made politics a dirty word, though in public relations, the same persons who would call politics dirty in private would use politics and their political contacts (hesitatingly or out of compulsion) to get their private work done. It is this kind of widespread social acceptability of political corruption that is responsible for its rapid spread or for making it self-reinforcing, because it makes both the politician and the prospective beneficiary of political corruption easily ready and willing.

It needs to be admitted that political corruption can be neither precisely measured nor even precisely defined. For, it is not easy to say what is a corrupt practice and what is not, or what is the proper and what is the improper use of authority, or what constitutes a departure from political norms. But such difficulties of definition are not peculiar to the concept of political corruption alone. They afflict other concepts as well, such as the concept of liquidity or of true depreciation in economics. Yet, apart from borderline cases, most other cases of political corruption can be easily identified as such. The problem of measurement (of the size and growth of political corruption) is much more intractable, as reliable information on the subject is hard to come by, most of the transactions being under the table.

Political corruption in India has infected political functionaries (broadly defined) at all levels, high or low. From the top of the hierarchy, comprising government ministers, legislators, senior bureaucrats, senior judges, senior police officers, senior officers of the armed forces and top office-bearers of the ruling party to the intermediate as well as lower levels—at the centre as well as the states and districts and the bottom of local government in cities, towns and villages and their corresponding political functionaries—corruption is quite widespread and common. Exceptions, of course, exist. But their number at all levels has declined considerably in recent years. Further, judging by the amount of bribes involved, corruption, on an average, is higher at the higher levels of the political hierarchy and lower as we go down the hierarchy. Again, there would be exceptions, as some government officials and other political functionaries are specially adept at extracting bribes even at the lower levels than others at the higher levels. In a highly imperfect and unorganised market for corruption, this is bound to happen. Also, not all the government functionaries occupy places of equal potential for doing private good or harm to the members of the public, and especially to the rich clientele. Therefore, the opportunity as well as the temptation and also the pressures for indulging in extortion of bribes vary a good deal across places and positions and are not the same across the board. That is why government employees often compete among themselves for their postings to relatively more lucrative positions and places and even bribe the higher officials, ministers, legislators or party leaders for such positings. Bribes for such postings in tax departments (income tax, excise, customs and sales tax), the public works department, police, for recruitment into the armed and security forces, for desired transfers or stays, and so on, are fairly common.

The foregoing brief account suggests an important distinction: that between what I would call 'primary corruption' and 'secondary corruption'. I shall call corruption in 'high places' primary corruption and corruption in intermediate and low positions secondary corruption. My hypothesis is that it is primary corruption which induces as well as tolerates secondary corruption so that practically the whole political system comes to suffer from it. This occurs because, in a hierarchical structure, authority flows from the top towards the bottom, so that the lower rungs of the ladder have no control over the behaviour of the higher rungs, but the reverse holds. If the higher-ups indulge in corruption, they set a bad example for the lower-downs to follow; they also lose their moral authority over their subordinates. Thus, the demonstration effect and the loss of moral authority combine to spread corruption at the lower levels, too. The economic pressure exerted by 'repressed inflation' on the fixed-income group of government employees and their ever-growing relative poverty vis-à-vis black-income earners, and their resulting appetite for riches even by corrupt means do the rest, that is, accelerate the spread process. The result is all-round political corruption.

If this argument is largely correct, it follows that for reducing political corruption, a beginning will have to be made at the top and in a demonstrable way, so that the message of anti-corruption spreads horizontally as well as vertically below. The anti-corruption drive will also have to be fairly sustained and of reasonably wide coverage to attain a certain degree of success because, by now, the disease of corruption has become so widespread and socially acceptable that it has come to characterise the normal behaviour pattern and functioning of most political functionaries.

Factors Determining Political Corruption

The most important ultimate factors responsible for generating as well as encouraging political corruption (and so black operations) in the Indian socio-economic-political setting are discussed briefly in this section. They lie at the root of most sources and forms of political corruption. They may be distinguished from what may be called proximate factors, which are specific to particular sources of political corruption (and black operations) and are true in the first instance or on the surface. These factors will be illustrated in the next two chapters.

Social Structure

In a capitalist society, political corruption is structurally determined, in the sense that the prevailing structure of social relations both generates the demand for and the supply of it.

It is a well-worked-out proposition of the theory of Marxist sociology that in a 'capitalist social formation,' the capitalist mode of production based on private property in the means of production determines the main axis of social structure (see Poulantzas, 1973). A full-scale discussion of this proposition will take us too far afield. Therefore, only a very brief explanation of it is offered here.

According to Marxist theory, a social formation is the historical outcome of the working of several overlapping modes and forms of production in various stages of their development. Correspondingly, at any time, there are several social classes, fractions and strata comprising the social formation. Further, such a formation is always the outcome of the working out of all the distinct, though interconnected, factors—economic, political, ideological and cultural—over a long period of time. A social formation carries with it the label of its dominant mode of production, which throws immense light on the character of social relations constituting the formation. Thus, a social formation with the capitalist mode of production (CMP) as the dominant mode is called the 'capitalist social formation' (CSF). The CMP identifies the unique character of the relations of production organised around the private ownership of the (large) means of production (indicating relations of property) and worked with free wage labour hired in the labour market. Its dominance indicates that the bulk of capital accumulation (extended reproduction of capital)—the key dynamic factor in the social formation—is undertaken under the CMP.

Even with the dominance of the CMP, but the simultaneous presence (or survival) of the pre-capitalist modes of production, there will be a vast ocean of other classes and groups, collectively called 'petty bourgeoisie' in Marxian theory, and 'middle classes' more generally. Often, a weak or strong class alliance develops among capitalists and large landowners under the ideological as well as political hegemony of large capital or of the capitalist state.

As a result of the dominance of the CMP in the CSF, on the demand side of the market for political corruption, we have in such a social formation economically dominant classes which stand to gain highly from extra political favours bestowed on them (in the form of, say, government supply and construction contracts, industrial and foreign exchange licenses, quotas, subsidies, favourable tax treatment, and preferential allocation of bank credit. Also, in general, the wealthier a business house or the larger the amount of assets it controls, the greater its capacity to absorb benefits from government favours, thereby making the demand for special political favours a rising function of the assets a business house already controls. In comparison, the poor do not have a material base on which to raise their claims for large political favours. At best, they can erect *jhuggies* (small huts for living) on vacant plots of land or engage in petty crimes of pick-pocketing and small thefts or act as carrier boys or peddlers of drugs, illicit liquor, smuggling, and so on, and even join the ranks of terrorists and other criminals.

On the supply side of the market for political corruption, the structure determines the 'ruling political elite' or the 'class-in-charge' of the state and the ruling political party. In the Indian context, they are fractions of the urban intermediate classes and of large landowners and middle farmers who occupy the top and middle level places in several state apparatuses and ruling political parties. This elite is either instrumental in awarding directly state favours in demand or in making political arrangements for the bestowal of such awards. Given this, transactional alliances or other arrangements develop between the demanders and the suppliers of political favours, either directly or indirectly through intermediaries. The demanders of political favours may even be foreign manufacturers or suppliers (for instance, of defence equipment) or big contractors (such as, for laying down gas pipelines). Each such government contract is usually of a very high value of hundreds of crore of rupees. Since the middleman's commission, kickback or bribe is usually a certain percentage of the value of the order (and not a fixed sum), usually payable in the currency of one's choice, the amount of pay-off for any big government order usually runs into several crore rupees. Therefore, in the context of the charge of corruption in high places in certain defence deals (such as the Bofors guns or the HDW German submarines that rocked the Indian parliament during 1986 and 1987), it was even argued in the press that such kickbacks had become the most important source of the ruling party political funds—more important than even the traditional source of company contributions.

Thus, the structure determines the main parties to political corruption—the capitalists as the main demanders and potential beneficiaries of political favours and political functionaries as the sellers of political favours. The structure also determines the forms of political corruption, too numerous to be recounted here. We may only say that the capitalist character of the state greatly facilitates interaction between capitalists and political functionaries, including the senior bureaucracy, such that the forms of favours and bribes are suitably designed to meet the requirements of the parties to the bargain and minimise chances of easy detection. As already mentioned, government employees on the lower rungs of the bureaucratic hierarchy also indulge in bribe-taking, depending on the extent to which they (and their office colleagues) deal with the public and with their actions, fair and foul, can favour or harm the interests of particualr members of the society they are dealing with.

Political corruption is not peculiar to capitalist societies. It is found in socialist societies as well. However, the form, practice, basis and the participating groups in the two types of societies are peculiar to each social formation and its historical development. In particular, the political factor counts for much more in socialist countries (as exemplified starkly by the communist countries of eastern Europe and erstwhile USSR) than it does in capitalist societies. Our object here is not to offer a generalised discussion of political corruption, but of it only with respect to the Indian experience of the post-Independence period.

State Intervention

The opportunities for political corruption are an increasing function of state intervention, other things being the same. State intervention defines the reach of the state in economic matters through state regulation and the control of economic activity. One common property of state regulation and controls is that they operate by raising formal barriers against the free flow of resources into designated economic activities and by imposing formal restrictions/conditions on production, distribution and prices of selected commodities. It is usually claimed that the state does all this in the national interest and to safeguard the interests of the weaker sections. State regulations and controls are also defended in the name of planning and to serve several ends of policy, concerned with the allocation of resources, capacity creation and utilisation, fair product distribution and pricing, checking the concentration of economic power, and so on.

However, we must also take note of the dark side of the picture. Among other things, this has to do with the accompanying political corruption and black operations. The simplest explanation is this. Market barriers tend to create a sellers market and scarcity rents in the concerned industries. Often, these scarcity rents or abnormal (actual and expected) profits serve as a magnet for most businessmen, and they use a variety of methods, both scrupulous and unscrupulous, to cross the official barriers by bending or breaking them, with or without the collusion of the state personnel at various levels. Their complete listing is not an easy task. For our purpose, it is sufficient to note that state regulation and controls have offered umpteen opportunities for political corruption to the unscrupulous. Political corruption has also vitiated the setting up and running of the public sector undertakings.

However, it is not purely interventions of the state in economic matters that are a source of political corruption. Even the liberal (non-interventionist) state which requires raising and spending of public revenues for civil administration, defence, public works, and so on, offers opportunities for political corruption, tax evasion and other black operations. State int rvention in economic matters only enhances the sweep of state activities and, therewith, the opportunities for political corruption and black operations.

What is increased state intervention due to? No single factor is responsible. Speaking analytically, two opposite forces of demand and supply for state intervention have reinforced each other. The demand for state intervention has come from practically all the social classes—from the subordinate classes for the alleviation of poverty, destitution and unemployment and for better living conditions; from the dominant bourgeois classes for the creation of more and more favourable conditions for capital accumulation through such measures as the rapid and adequate development of infrastructural and basic and heavy industries, protection to domestic industry against foreign competition, favourable fiscal policy incorporating tax concessions and subsidies in favour of investment in physical capital, and favourable credit allocation policy. Individual capitalists have competed among themselves for the grant of licenses, quotas, approval of foreign collaboration, and so on. Each of these government permissions has carried a large amount of premium or rent, which their demanders or private beneficiaries have been happy to share with the suppliers of such state permissions in various forms.

On the supply side, the political elite has been very keen to extend the scope of state intervention. The ostensible purpose has been the promotion of all-round economic development of the country and the welfare of the weaker sections of society under the active direction or participation of the state. All this has been generally welcome to state and party functionaries, as each expansion of state intervention generally enhances their power over the economy and society, and so the opportunities to extract rent from the beneficiaries of state favours.

Thus, there are powerful social forces on both the demand and supply sides operating to reproduce and even extend state intervention.

High Political Anomie

Webster's dictionary has defined the term 'anomie' "as a state of society in which normative standards of conduct and belief are weak or lacking". Durkheim (1970), who is credited with introducing the term in sociology, had stressed that the concept of anomie further implied an inadequacy of forces—both at the individual and the collective or institutional level—*to regulate appetites, behaviour and social life*. It also implies serious disorientation in political life. For the concrete Indian case, Manor (1983) has interpreted anomie as a departure from *norms, values and constraints which had substantial influence in political life between 1947 and the mid-1960s*. After this period (the Nehru period) and especially since the early 1970s, anomic forces have progressively gained ground in India's political life. Manor (1983) has discussed 'anomie in Indian politics' entirely in terms of the breakdown or decay of the Congress party as India's central political institution and its main instrument for conflict management, and not brought in the parallel decay of India's state and its several apparatuses, especially the government, its administration (the civil services or the bureaucracy), the police and the judiciary. But, political anomie has proceeded on all these fronts.

Very importantly, political anomie has afflicted the entire political system through political corruption and black operations. In fact, political anomie lies at the root of political corruption. Very briefly, it may be explained thus: politics offers a lot of opportunities to its practioners to make quick money through the sale of state favours and patronage; state intervention enhances the scope of such opportunities; given the large demand for state favours, when the barriers of norms and values grow weak or are lacking in a system (or regime), anomic (normless) political functionaries fall easy prey to temptations of political corruption; further, a lack of constraint on their appetite for riches pushes them headlong in the same direction. It, then, follows that the greater the anomie in a political system, the larger also the political corruption in it. Therefore, at times, the two terms (political anomie and political corruption) are mentioned synonymously. But, analytically, the former is the cause of which the latter is an effect.

Possibly, the best concrete way of comprehending political anomie is to identify its objective expression in the form of decay of political institutions and practices and the rise of a new breed of politicians, some of whom have also captured the power of the state and who, at best, are self-servers with large appetites. The decay of political institutions and practices is associated with at least two developments in the political field: (*a*) deinstitutionalisation of the Congress party (see Rudolph and Rudolph, 1987, Chapter 4), the dominant all-India party; and (*b*) decline in parliamentary institutions, conventions and practices and rise in the power of the executive (the government) and the bureaucracy. Thereby even indirect accountability of the government to the people through their elected representatives has been marginalised. This has adversely affected the content of political democracy in the country, one horrendous expression of which was the imposition of national Emergency (1975–77) in the country. (For a fuller discussion, see Manor, 1983 and Rudolph and Rudolph, 1987.)

Very briefly, at the level of the Congress party, the beginning of the process of political anomie has been basically the result of a particular style of response of the main political actors of the Congress party in the tussle for domination in the party between the 'syndicate' of five party bosses (as 'king makers'), on the one hand, and Indira Gandhi (as the Prime Minister of India), on the other hand. In this intra-party struggle, the corporate interests of the party were sacrificed at the altar of personal survival and domination of the party and the government by Indira Gandhi. The Congress party was split vertically first in 1969 and then again in 1978. Indira Gandhi emerged as the supreme undisputed leader of her part of the divided Congress. She built up a new and totally changed Congress, personally loyal to her, each important member of which owed his or her position and power in the party or the government to her personally. Further, she secured for herself the image of a radical and progressive leader and the only true friend of the poor and the downtrodden in the Congress party and the government. She did this with the help of such popular and populist measures as the nationalisation of fourteen large Indian commercial banks (in 1969) and the abolition of the privy purses of the princes of the erstwhile Indian states (in 1970). *Garibi hatao* (remove poverty) was used as the key slogan of the mid-term 1971 parliamentary elections, converting it into a virtual plebiscite around her personal leadership and policies. The resounding victory in the 1971 parliamentary elections, followed by victory in the state assembly elections later, were attributed to her personal charisma and following among the voters.

These victories freed Indira Gandhi from the constraints of party organisation and procedures on the decision-making processes at the national as well as state levels. She began to circumvent or ignore them. This rendered the party organisation as well as the Parliament (with a large Congress party majority) practically unimportant, if not redundant. Indira Gandhi came to be regarded as the greatest asset with the Congress party for winning elections and the key to political power and advancement for individual aspirants. In the ensuing climate of sycophancy, personal loyalty, not party commitment, became the touchstone for survival as well as promotion in the party and also the government. Even respected party leaders of long-standing had to declare such loyalty publicly. What was true of the party was equally true of the government, where the ministry at the centre was shuffled much too often, adding new faces and dropping a few old ones. Similarly, the chief ministers in the Congress-majority states were nominated by Indira Gandhi and continued to stay in power under her pleasure. In the process, the legislative wing of the government got downgraded in comparison with its executive wing and the bureaucracy.

The result was the demise of 'mediated politics,' that is, politics mediated through political parties and the deinstitutionalisation of the Congress party. The policy-making processes of the government came to be handled by Indira Gandhi and her confidants alone; the sense of public participation in the government decision-making processes was diminished greatly.

Two additional factors that led to the deinstitutionalisation of the Congress party were the total dismantling of intra-party democracy and the entry of socially undesirable elements in the party, wielding much political clout through party and government forums. Periodic organisational elections to elect office bearers at various levels of the party remained suspended from 1972 and all the senior party posts were filled by nominations from the top. In most cases, the chief ministers were nominated by Indira Gandhi herself (and later by Rajiv Gandhi) for their personal loyalty to her(him) as their first essential qualification. Such chief ministers remained more dependent on her favour and pleasure than the support of representative bodies. She smothered ruthlessly any potential challenge to her supreme leadership of the Congress party and did not like her colleagues to command independent strong political bases of their own. So, no political collegiality for her and no competing centres of power. She was herself the president of (her part of) the Congress party and, after her assasination in October 1984, her elder son and political heir, Rajiv Gandhi, assumed the two offices of the Congress presidentship and India's prime ministership.

Another feature of the malaise has concerned the method and quality of candidate selection for party posts at various levels, as well as for elections to Parliament at the Centre and several of the state assemblies. It has ceased to be a principled party process. Instead, personal loyalty to Indira Gandhi became a basic qualification for candidate selection. This kept better-quality potential candidates with high ability and probity out of the political arena. Those who came up instead in the party and the government were persons for whom politics was an occupation—more a career and a way to make a living, to gain power and riches, than a cause worthy of service and sacrifice. This kind of candidate selection was accelerated and deepened during the meteoric rise of Sanjay Gandhi, especially during the Emergency regime (1975–77). The Sanjay followers, who catapulted into the national limelight as Youth Congress activists, even overshadowed for a time seasoned Congress party leaders and workers. Most of them who were given party tickets for the elections, in the name of youth, were brash young men, inexperienced, ignorant of the world of mediated politics, parliamentary norms and conventions, prone to disrupt legislatures and to agitational action. Some who rode the Congress bandwagon were even persons with criminal records and tendencies. In subsequent elections, the number of unsavoury candidates has gone up with increased poll violence and booth-capturing. Some of them have got elected, too. As a result, the overall quality of political life and the quality of leadership in the country's Parliament, state legislatures and the government has suffered much decline. Things were no better during the short-lived non-Congress rule at the Centre (1990–91). The resulting political anomie has encouraged all-round political and administrative corruption.

Contributions to Party Funds

A political party is not a business organisation engaged in some commercial activity and making money from it. It is a political organisation designed to render political services to the people without any fee or charge. It does not own any revenue-yielding assets either. But it needs funds or material support to carry on and finance its day-to-day activities, travels and daily expenses of its fulltime office-bearers and workers, regular organisational functions, expenses of its special sessions and, most importantly, for meeting the expenses of fighting elections. The latter have become increasingly expensive, partly because of greater reliance on highly expensive media and methods of electioneering, buying of votes, decline in the proportion of honest and selfless party workers and increase in the role of mercenaries in the party organisation who try to make money for themselves from every occasion and opportunity. They are professionals with large appetites for private riches and use their party positions and influence in the party and the government for extracting bribes for themselves along with contributions and material support to the party. This kind of material support comes in various forms. For example, during the election campaign and on election days, interested companies and persons are known to provide free services of fleets of vehicles with patrol and drivers, free sumptuous refreshment and entertainment to party workers, and free publicity material.

The political bribing of party and government elites is a pervasive and continuous affair. It is sanctioned by party practices of raising funds from all sorts of sources, most of which represent unaccounted money. For example, they may be mills which raise such money from the under-reporting of their true output and thereby save on excise duty, corporation tax and personal income tax, selling unreported output in the open (black) market, with the entire extra gain going only to the management and not shared with the company shareholders. Other sources of party finance may be smugglers and other tax-evaders.

Theoretically, therefore, for the ruling political party, there need be no dearth of financial resources, if the party leaders are willing to enter into an exchange alliance with 'money-bags' who would supply the party as well as its elites funds in exchange for various kinds of state favours. The 'money-bags' can be corporations who may or may not be allowed to make company contribtuions to political parties, smugglers, dealers in drugs or narcotics, tax evaders and other private individuals engaged in illegal activities. Company contributions to political parties were banned in 1969 and reallowed in 1985. Such contributions in large sums are often made in order to cultivate political influence, especially in the ruling political party and in the government of the day, to gain licenses, special quotas and permissions, government contracts, and tax concessions and reliefs. All such transactional alliances promote political corruption directly. Besides, if the party accepts tainted money as contributions to it, it tries its best to protect its sources of finance by suppressing all manner of information about them. The same applies with greater force in respect of individual party barons who fatten themselves on the counter-favours showered on them by the black-income earners. They build up huge reserves of privately-owned and controlled funds (through, say, tax-free public trusts and charities), which serve as a very important bulwark of their personal power and following in the party and the government.

Keeping in view the importance of money in electoral politics, it has been suggested in some quarters that the approved election expenses of the candidates of the recognised national and regional political parties should be treated as an essential expense of the democratic form of government and that certain approved amounts of such expenses should be met by the public exchequer. The allocation of funds could be done, say, on the strength of votes per party candidate polled by a party in a particular constituency (or state) in the previous election. The suggestion, however, has never been taken seriously by policy-makers, possibly because of the large financial burden it will impose on the state and also because the ruling party is not as short of funds as the opposition parties. Further, party fund-raisers do not like it, because they do not want to lose a very important basis of their clout in the party and with the financiers. However, the suggesion, if implemented, will not necessarily check entirely the use of undeclared private funds in elections, which will continue to vitiate the whole election process though, when combined with a more awakened and better organised electorate, the influence of money power in elections can be reduced substantially.

3

Sources of Black Income: I

Evasion of Income Tax

This section examines the evasion of income tax, both personal income tax and corporation (income) tax. I shall not go into a discussion of the evasion of other direct taxes, such as wealth tax, gift tax and estate duty (abolished in April 1965), because they contribute only a small amount to the total direct tax revenue of the government. (In 1988–89, this contribution was only Rs 122 crore from tax on wealth and Rs 7 crore from gift tax in the total direct tax revenue of Rs 8,644 crore.)

In the theory of public finance and in academic as well as policy discussions, much emphasis is laid on income tax. It is identified as a potent tool for correcting gross inequality in the personal distribution of income, characterised by gross disparities in the interpersonal distribution of wealth in general, and productive assets in particular. But, largely due to large-scale evasion of income tax (and of other taxes), the aforesaid goal of reduced inequality in the distribution of income and wealth has remained confined to only policy statements and has not been realised in practice. In fact, most observers of the Indian scene, not taken in by the measurement exercises of 'Gini coefficient' at the national level as an indicator of the prevailing degree of distributional inequality, are of the view that the inequality in the economy has grown, if anything.

The relative importance of income tax in the total tax revenue of the government may be gauged from the following figures for the financial year 1988–89. (Figures within brackets show the respective percentage of revenue from a particular tax to the total tax revenue.) The total tax revenue (including the states' share of income tax and Union excise duties) was Rs 44,419 crore. Of this amount, the yield from personal income tax, including surcharge, was Rs 4,237 crore (9.5 per cent), and from corporation (income) tax (including surcharge) was Rs 4,407 crore (9.9 per cent). In comparison, the contribution of excise duties was Rs 18.841 crore (42.4 per cent), and another Rs 15.805 crore (35.6 per cent) was raised through customs duties (net). The tax revenues from corporation tax go entirely to the Central government. However, those from personal income tax are shared by the Centre with the states. Thus, in 1988–89, of the total income-tax receipts of Rs 4,237 crore, Rs 2,749 crore was distributed among the states, with the Centre retaining only Rs 1,488 crore. The latter was inclusive of surcharge on personal income tax, all of which is appropriated by the Centre.

Two special features of personal as well as corporate income tax in India may be noted briefly here. First, during the past several years before 1985–86, the tax rates for both personal and corporate income tax have been on the high side. This feature has been held as one of the main factors responsible for high tax evasion in India. I shall examine this argument later in this section. Second, personal and corporate income tax are very highly complicated, surrounded as they are by a large number of exemptions and deductions and detailed conditions governing them. The latter are modified, clarified or elaborated upon very frequently through hundreds of lengthy notifications issued every year. All this has converted income tax law into a veritable jungle. Despite this, or because of this, exemptions and deductions bristle with several loopholes, which are expioited fully by rich businessmen with the help of legal services and bribes to tax officials, false accounts, and so on, to reduce substantially their tax liabilities.

Methods of Tax Evasion

Apart from salaries as a source of income in the organised sector where deduction of income tax at source is compulsory, in respect of almost all other sources of income, tax-evasion is nearly universal. The main methods used are discussed briefly below.

Suppression of True Income: This is the main method of tax evasion. A large part of black income is made by black operators through illegitimate means, in the form of bribes, smuggling of goods, black marketing, suppression of true excisable output (for the evasion of excise duty), suppression of sales (for the evasion of sales tax), underinvoicing of imports, under-declaration of the sale price of real estate, and so on. The income earned through these methods is clearly unreportable income. A large part of the income earned through otherwise legitimate means is also not reported to income-tax authorities, so as to evade tax on it. Such suppression of income also is widespread. Examples are provided by film stars and film producers, self-employed professionals (such as medical practitioners, lawyers, architects and chartered accountants), and persons engaged in business (trade and industry, including small-scale industry, construction, real estate and road transport). In most of these activities, regular accounts of business are either not maintained or they are false or manipulated accounts (called No. 2 accounts in common parlance). Therefore, even through income-tax raids it is very difficult to get sufficient evidence admissible in a court of law to convict the accused.

Overstatement of Business Expenditure: Another common method used is to overstate practically all items of business expenditure and to support the accounts with fictitious vouchers and entries in books. It is also common practice to live off the expense account of business (especially in respect to local transport, telephone services, entertainment, and so on, for the entire family). It is well-known that even the expenditure on lavish dinner parties at social ceremonies (such as a marriage or a birthday celebration in the family) is met on business account in various ways.

Abuse of Tax Concessions—Exemptions and Deductions: Several kinds of exemptions and deductions are permitted under the law. Instead of discussing them in full, I shall illustrate my argument with the help of two exemptions. One makes income from agriculture totally free from income tax, irrespective of the amount of income one makes on the farm. This opens up the possibility for rich persons in cities to buy and operate agricultural land and claim high agricultural profits—much higher than the actual—from agricultural operations, whereas most of these profits might have been from non-agricultural operations and hence taxable. (Agricultural income in such cases is added to non-agricultural income only to determine the marginal income-tax rate on the latter, but is not taxed itself.) Another example is that of basic exemption, making income above it alone a part of net taxable income. Taking advantage of this, a very large number of self-employed persons (such as, small traders) escape the tax net by creating several separate tax units in the family or simply by not filing income-tax returns, even though their income in most cases is far above the basic exemption. It is only through intensive surveys and searches that such tax-evaders can be brought to book and made to pay the tax.

It may be noted that exemptions/deductions have added immensely to the complexity of tax laws, which is taken full advantage of primarily by the rich, with assistance from specialist tax lawyers and income-tax officials, who have been suitably bribed. Further, exemptions/deductions are not equitable—they are heavily weighed in favour of wealthy investors, big agriculturists and big industrialists as against small entrepreneurs. This has promoted concentration of economic power in the country. Therefore, it is necessary to have proper safeguards through ceilings on selected exemptions and deductions, eliminating some and rationalising each one of them.

Tax Disputes and Tax Arrears: It has become increasingly popular with rich assessees to question tax assessments, go in for appeal against them and raise various objections. The objective of entering into disputes, among other things, is, first, to delay tax payment for as long as possible (and thereby to gain an interest-free loan from the government of the funds assessed by the income-tax authorities to be payable) and, second, to try all sorts of means (including money and political pressures and bribes) for a substantial reduction in tax to be paid finally.

This has already given birth to the serious problem of income-tax arrears, which was also examined carefully by the Wanchoo Committee (see Chapter 4). Over time, there has been a progressive increase in the amount of tax arrears outstanding and a continuous fall in the percentage of realisations to outstandings. The amount of tax arrears, which had stood at Rs 841 crore at the end of March 1970, had grown to more than Rs 3,500 crore twenty years later when individual arrears of less than Rs 10 lakh each were not counted in the latter. A large part of this increase, no doubt, is attributable to the multi-fold increase in money incomes, especially during recent years. But this does not affect the arrears (in money terms) carried forward from earlier years. Further, it is surmised that a significant increase in arrears is also due to the continuous increase in tax disputes and the use of other methods designed for tax evasion. It is worth noting that in 1969–70, whereas our tax collections were only about 50 per cent of current demand, the proportion of uncollected tax was only 9 per cent in the UK and the USA, and it was only around 4 per cent in Japan (Wanchoo Committee).

Benami (Fictitious) Dealings: *Benami* dealings abound greatly in the Indian economy. They are used to serve various ends, such as the evasion of land ceilings and taxes, and the conversion of black income and wealth into white income and wealth. Accordingly, the *benami* technique is practised widely in various fields of economic activity, such as the holding of agricultural land, urban land, stocks and shares, fixed deposits in banks and partnerships in firms. Even fictitious firms are set up, in whose name a part of business is conducted, bills and receipts issued and accepted. But, the firm exists only in name and on paper, without any separate physical presence of its own. In the period of acute shortages of essential goods in the past, when government quotas and permits commanded a high premium in the market and political contacts helped favourites in the procurement of these quotas and permits, even when they did not have any regular business establishments, the allottees of quotas and permits made a lot of money by simply selling these quotas and permits in the 'black market'. The profits so made, of course, remained undeclared for tax purposes, as the business firms in question would be totally fictitious.

In business, the use of 'fictitious bills' is very common and widespread. I have used the term fictitious bills broadly, to include several forms of bills, explained briefly here. Under one commonly-practised form, a seller sells only a bill to a buyer, without any corresponding delivery of goods or services as mentioned in the bill. Or, he may simply overbill his customer. In both cases, the buyer-businessman pays the full value of the bill by cheque and the seller refunds the excess to him in cash. Thereby, both the buyer and the seller gain. The buyer gains as he obtains a receipt for a deductible expense, which is used to reduce taxable profits artificially. The seller gains because, by showing fictitious sales, he brings revenue and profits 'into his books' and thus 'whitens' his black income, even if he has to pay some income tax on this 'fictitious income'. This technique is used by senior managers also (for purely personal gains), if they control directly the price of the products purchased by their establishments and themselves disburse payments to the suppliers of the products. (It is like a disbursing officer paying lower wages to the workers than what is entered in the wage register and what the worker puts his thumb impression against.) More generally, anyone with business and professional income and in need of whitening some black income or wealth may inflate his sales and profits against fictitious receipts and bring more income 'on to the books,' though at some incremental tax liability.

Underbilling of goods, including the sale of goods without a bill, is also quite common. The trader does it to under-report his sales and thereby save on sales tax as well as income tax, that is, evade partly the two taxes. The buyer may or may not gain on sales tax. As happens at times, the buyer pays the sales tax only if he insists on a sales receipt. In other cases, the price quoted by the trader may be inclusive of sales tax. Then, if the sales receipt is not made out, the trader pockets the sales tax also along with his regular profit margin. There are also small industries and trade that have thrived greatly on indirect-tax evasion. They sell and buy goods without a regular bill and a challan—on No. 2 (i.e., black transactions) account. Well-known examples of such industries and trade in Delhi are steel utensils, electrical goods and P.V.C. *chappals*. In the powerloom centres of Surat and Bhiwandi, excise duty on powerloom products is openly evaded. In all such cases, income tax also gets easily evaded.

Manipulations of stock market transactions serve as another significant avenue for black-income generation and for converting black into white. This is accomplished partly by doing business in fictitious names or in the names of dependents in the family (wife and children), and partly by doing unreportable business of buying and selling shares through a trusted broker who does not insist on the physical delivery of share certificates (both ways) and settles much of buy and sell business through the periodic cross cancellation of payments and receipts and requiring only the balance in the account to be settled in cash. Such business also is usually conducted in fictitious names.

Another device commonly used for tax evasion and for converting black into white are *hawala* loans. Such a loan is usually a fictitious loan, where the lender shown in books is a fictitious person, a friend or a relative. (The latter do not actually lend, but are only shown in name to have lent.) *Hawala* transactions are equally common in the market for foreign exchange, and serve as an important device for foreign exchange leakages. We shall study them later in the chapter.

Tax Avoidance

Tax avoidance, like tax evasion, also results in the loss of tax revenue. But there is an important distinction between the two—whereas the former is legal, the latter is not. In other words, the distinction rests on the difference between the methods of escape from the tax liability resorted to. True tax avoidance simply avails of tax exemptions or tax privileges provided by the government strictly in accordance with law and so is legitimate, while tax evasion involves the use of illegitimate methods. But, in practice, in the name of tax planning, such methods and practices are frequently used to reduce the tax burden and to circumvent the law in its spirit and intent, though without technically violating the law. No law can be perfectly foolproof. In fact, the rules governing the scope of a particular exemption or the grant of a particular tax incentive may suffer from certain loopholes (for examples, see Bagchi, 1974). Already, attempts to plug loopholes in rule-making have made the tax laws more and more complicated, but without much success in checking unwarranted tax avoidance. This has also led to tax disputes, where even the high courts are not credited with consistent decisions (again, for examples, see Bagchi, 1974). Tax-avoidance efforts, with the help of tax lawyers, have even resulted in spurious claims made for tax benefits and the manipulation of accounts, including fraud, that borders on tax evasion. In fact, spurious tax avoidance is a first cousin of tax evasion and serves as one of its tools.

I shall now discuss the commonly-used methods of tax-avoidance in India.

Tax Expenditures: Such expenditures (also called tax subsidies) represent government financial assistance to business, extended through the tax system in the form of special tax concessions/deductions and not directly through the budget. This method of tax expenditure is widely practised in India. Yet, there is continuous pressure for more of it through their extension to newer areas of economic activity and their enlargement in existing areas. Almost every government committee and study group, in its recommendations, religiously includes new tax deductions as an incentive without undertaking any cost-benefit analysis of its recommendations.

Two illustrations of such expenditures are given here. The major one is the 'investment allowance', operative since 1976 (withdrawn from 1 April 1991). (Earlier, 'Development rebate' had operated from 1 April 1955 to 31 May 1974 and was of considerable assistance to Indian industry.) The investment allowance had been available at the rate of 25 per cent of the cost of new ship or new aircraft acquired or new plant or machinery installed. Where plant or machinery is installed for control of pollution or for the protection of environment or for the manufacture of indigenously developed articles, the investment allowance was 35 per cent. The other example is provided by 'tax holidays'. In 1984, a complete tax holiday for five years was available for newly established industrial undertakings in free trade zones, while new industrial undertakings, hotels, and so on, established anywhere in India have been entitled to claim a tax-holiday benefit equal to 2.5 per cent of their income for eight years. For new industrial undertakings and hotels established in backward areas, this benefit has been available for ten years, and equal to 20 per cent of profits. There are several other provisions in the Indian tax system that have also enabled companies to generate handsome tax savings (for examples, see Gupta 1984a: M107.)

What is admissible under a particular deduction and what is not is defined by detailed rules (framed by the bureaucracy) accompanying a particular sub-section. This has made the tax laws extremely complicated and generally incomprehensible. It is no wonder that the demand for the services of tax-expert lawyers has been going up rapidly. Despite or because of the voluminous rules/conditions governing the large number of deductions and exemptions, there is much scope for filing spurious claims for tax deductions on various counts, mainpulation of accounts and tax disputes with tax authorities. Thus, the provision for tax expenditures is openly misused as a tool of tax evasion. What proportion of tax expenditures is so used is hard to say. But that tax expenditures have gone to benefit large companies the most is well supported by empirical evidence. Some of it is mentioned below.

For the financial year 1982–83, the studies conducted by the *Economic Times* (and published in its issues of 4 April and 2 May 1984) had shown that 84 private sector corporate giants in India with profits before tax of Rs 416 crore had reported a tax liability of a mere Rs 1.3 crore (for further details, see Gupta, 1984b: M127.) A study by the Industrial Credit and Investment Corporation of India (1984) had also revealed that, for the financial year 1982–83, out of the 338 profit-making companies covered by the study, 153 companies belonged to the category of 'zero-tax companies'. Despite this kind of empirical evidence, the Federation of Indian Chambers of Commerce and Industry (FICCI), the chief mouthpiece of organised industry in India, and other business organisations never tire of stressing the point that the tax burden on industry in India is top heavy, that there are not enough tax incentives, and that more tax relief should be given to industry to promote a faster rate of industrial development of the country.

Furthermore, Gupta (1984b: M123-M27) has pointed out that the *All India Income Tax Statistics* (AIITS) brought out by the Ministry of Finance, Government of India, suffers from serious failings and inaccuracies in the publication of the relevant data. In particular, the AIITS data do not cover the deductions allowed in respect of the development rebate (1955–74) or even the investment allowance (since 1976), when it is well-known that these deductions have been a major item of tax expenditure in India. In addition, the AIITS data on income-tax deductions are highly unreliable. As such, they are a source of much disinformation as they give the totally false impression that the tax relief provided through income-tax deductions does not amount to much, whereas the truth is just the opposite.

The damage being done to the public attitude and awareness

due to the aforesaid disinformation is enormous. The common refrain is that the tax structure in India is highly oppressive and obstructive of growth. In the words of Bagchi (1974: 953):

> even in most of the expert writings, stylised models are set up to show how the tax rates depress the yield to make it unremunerative to work, save or invest, with little regard to the presence of the sumptuous exemptions and deductions that are available to taxpayers of most categories.

After all, these concessions mean a loss of tax revenue to the government, additional administrative cost for ensuring the proper compliance of tax laws and increased scope for tax evasion and spurious avoidance. In any scheme of tax reform, it seems best to totally do away with tax expenditures and lower significantly the corporate tax rate.

Hindu Undivided Family (HUF)

Another device for tax avoidance commonly used by rich Hindu families is that of HUF as a separate tax unit—a feature peculiar to the direct taxation of Hindu joint families in India. The studies of Gulati and Gulati (1962) and Gulati (1973) throw much useful light on the subject. I shall draw from them liberally here.

Under HUF, a Hindu family comprising at least two assessees (not husband and wife) can claim the status of an HUF for tax purposes, with some commonly-owned earning assets. This is done only to take certain tax advantages. These flow primarily from two sources. One is the splitting of income and wealth. Under the Indian tax laws, an HUF is treated as a separate tax unit—separate from the individual assessees that compose it. (This is true of personal income tax as well as wealth tax.) As such, each one is entitled to a separate exemption limit as well as a tax rate schedule applicable to it.

However, this alone is a minor source of tax avoidance. It has been multiplied several-fold in a number of ways. First, an HUF can be divided and subdivided into smaller units of HUFs, each unit comprising a separate taxable unit with a separate exemption limit (see also the third point below). Second, an HUF has access to 'partial' partition, so that while the HUF properties can be partially divided amongst its individual members, the HUF can still retain its distinct identity. Thus, when a family partitions some of the properties among its members, while the income of the partitioned properties is added to the income of the individual members from their self-acquired properties or from sources unrelated to family assets, the income from the undivided properties can be shown separately as HUF income for tax purposes, and the law provides no means of assessing the two incomes together even if they are received and enjoyed by the same individual. Third, the persons who are parties to the original partition (partial or complete) may reunite into one or more HUFs as and when desired. It is not necessary that such reunions be among *all* the members of the original HUF or that *all* the assets received by the reuniting members at the time of original partition be pooled back. In fact, as illustrated by Gulati (1973), a small HUF consisting of a widower father and three adult, but unmarried, sons can form as many as ten HUF assessment units and, at the same time, have four individual assessment units. This conjecture was supported fully by the studies commissioned by the Wanchoo Committee (1971: 74–75).

The device of HUF (with partial partitioning) is now more widely used than before for tax avoidance. Thus, whereas the number of taxable HUFs in 1967–68 was 73,750, twenty years later, in 1987–88, this number had grown to 172,740. The only effective and straightforward way to suitably plug the HUF route to tax avoidance seems to be the recommendations of the Raj Committee (1974) that the present recognition to the HUF as a separate unit of assessment should be withdrawn totally, and that each adult member of the HUF should be taxed only as an individual on the basis of his total income/wealth from all sources, including his share of HUF income/wealth.

Other Methods of Tax Avoidance: To save space, I shall examine other methods of tax avoidance rather briefly.

Clubbing of the Income of Spouse and Minor children: If the spouse or minor children do not have any independent source of income of their own, their incomes are clubbed with the income of the earning member (husband/father) in the family. To escape from this clubbing and to benefit from the existence of as many separate tax units in the family as possible (in the form of separate exemption limits and lower marginal tax rates), certain measures are commonly adopted. One essential step is to create a nucleus of assets of dependents in the family from outside sources. In the case of the wife, one common method is to claim that some of the assets are a part of her *stree dhan* (woman's wealth), which she had received from her parents (and others) at the time of her marriage. Then, she might have earned some money doing certain odd jobs in the service market. This claim may be supported by fake certificates. The device of gifts is open to all and also made much use of to provide a nucleus of assets for minor children. (For a fuller discussion, see the section on 'Gifts'.)

Once independent assets of the wife and minor children have been secured, each one of them is entitled to a separate exemption limit in her/his own right as an individual. Thus, in a family of five, with the exemption limit of Rs 22,000 and with proper tax planning, the family as a whole can enjoy a total exemption limit of Rs 110,000. Several families take full or partial advantage of this loophole in tax laws, and thereby reduce substantially their income-tax liability. One way to plug this loophole would be to treat the nuclear family unstead of the individual as the tax unit (see Sundaram and Pandit, 1979).

Charitable and Religious Trusts: Avoidance of tax through the medium of charitable and religious trusts is a common malady in serveral countries of the world, including India. For example, in India, public donations to such trusts, duly registered with the income-tax authorities, and incomes thereof, applied for approved public, religious or charitable purposes, are exempted from tax. This is done to promote philanthropic activities in the country. But such tax-exemptions are often greatly misused by the trustees. For example, studies for India have shown that business houses setting up trusts mostly appropriate trust funds for their own businesses and that, in several cases, trust properties and incomes are widely abused by the founders of trusts, trustees and their relatives. 'Black money' also is said to find its way to such trusts in the form of 'ghost' or anonymous donations. (With the tightening of the Income Tax Act and the Wealth Tax Act, this problem is now presumably not as serious as before.)

Gifts. I have already mentioned that the medium of gifts is commonly used by tax-payers to create a nucleus of assets of dependents in the family (non-working wife and minor children) in the form of gifts from outside donors. This helps reduce the tax liability of the nuclear family through the creation of separate tax units, claiming separate exemption limits and lower marginal tax rates. To curb such a practice, the Gift-Tax Act was passed in 1958, with a progressive tax-rate structure. The initial basic exemption limit of Rs 5,000 was later revised to Rs 10,000, and then again to Rs 20,000.

A major change in the taxation of gifts was proposed in the budget for 1990–91, and made effective from 20 March, 1990. Till then, gifts were taxed in the hands of the donor and there was no limit on the amount which a donee could show as having been received by way of gifts. Consequently, the mechanism of gifts was used to split up capital and launder black money. In some recent cases, attempts were made to explain away even wasteful and ostentatious expenditure on marriage receptions and other functions as having been financed out of gifts. To curb such practices, the gift-tax, based on donors has been replaced by a donee-based gift-tax, other things remaining unchanged. Gifts received in foreign exchange through official channels will remain exempt from tax. This is a serious lacuna. It has been exploited in the past on a big enough scale to convert black money into white money. To do so, black money is first sent abroad through, say, *hawala* transactions, and rupee funds are converted into foreign exchange at the going market rate of discount. The same funds are brought back into India openly through official channels as 'gifts'.

Faced with the severe foreign exchange crisis and the urgent need to attract foreign exchange into India, the State Bank of India, with the approval of the Central government and the RBI, floated NRI bonds (second series) in November 1990, with specially attractive features. They carry a high enough (11 per cent per year) rate of interest, loan facility and premature encashment facility, and can be gifted to any Indian individual or charitable trust. Also, these bonds are fully exempt from income, wealth and gift tax in India, even in the hands of donees. According to market reports, the new NRI bonds have served as a popular vehicle for converting black money into white money, apart from serving as a highly attractive paper for investment.

Factors Responsible for Tax Evasion

Several factors have been held responsible for tax evasion in India in discussions on the subject. This discussion is not a survey of these diverse explanations. Instead, I shall offer a systematic analysis of these factors under a few heads and in a manner consistent with the discussion in the rest of this book. I shall also concentrate on what I consider to be the most crucial factors.

Unrestrained Pursuit of Private Gains: The pursuit of private gains is universal. Combined with honest enterprise, it is one of the main sources of economic growth. But, for social harmony as well as social weal, it has to be subject to certain well-defined and well-accepted social constraints. (I am not talking here about the technological or production constraints or about the budget constraint.) The earlier restraints of social norms or responsibility or moral rectitude or professional honesty have weakened greatly. This is surely a sign of *civilisational crisis,* when the normless pursuit of wealth and power generates its own antithesis—not necessarily in the same field, but in sundry other fields, for instance, of the environment through the reckless destruction of forests, the increased production of air, water and atmospheric pollutants, and social conflicts and tension. Black income generation, the spread of the killer disease *AIDS*, trade in narcotic drugs, even the political dominance of the narco-mafia in some countries and their strong involvement in terrorism and social violence are all manifestations of the same civilisational crisis. Thus viewed, black incomes and tax evasion are only external symptoms of a deeper social malaise—of a social sickness that is fast eating into the vitals of the entire social system. Its consequences must be truly catastrophic, which only the complete restructuring of the whole economy, society, polity and culture can help avoid. As to leadership, it must be in the hands of persons of broad and deep social vision and commitment and of honest and truthful character.

Such a proper placement of the origin and growth of black economy in a wider social/civilisational context is essential for identifying its true causes and for devising ways and means whereby the evil can be checked and then gradually curtailed, if not rooted out completely. Presently, the remedies adopted are worse than the disease itself.

Various authorities on the subject of tax evasion have recognised the importance of the above factor. But, usually, the factor is couched in moral terms such as 'deterioration in moral standards' (Wanchoo Committee, 1971: 10) and not placed in the proper social context. Thereby, it loses much of its appeal.

Political Corruption: One concrete expression of the social malady discussed above is political corruption. Tax evasion and political corruption are inseparable and mutually reinforcing. One causes the other. Thus, tax evaders need protection against the rigors of law. Most of them also seek a share in the distribution of government largesse and patronage. Politicians and bureaucrats provide both, but only in return for appropriate economic rewards. I have already discussed the subject of political corruption at length in Chapter 2. Here, I shall only say that political corruption makes the social fight against black income and tax evasion several times more difficult than otherwise. This is because, in today's world, politics is the main weapon for fighting social ills and when the main weapon itself gets blunted by political corruption, the chances of winning the aforesaid fight become that much bleaker—a social tragedy.

Corrupt Business Practices: Another concrete expression of the unrestrained pursuit of private gains is the proliferation of corrupt business practices in the country. I have called them black operations. This book is full of instances of black operations in various fields of economic activity and also offers a systematic analysis of them. I shall only add that many of the corrupt business practices lead to an ever-increasing need for black funds, even on the part of otherwise-honest businessmen as, for instance, for the payment of secret commissions, bribes, and *pugree* or black funds in real estate transactions. Such payments invariably act as the mechanism for the spread of corrupt business practices throughout the economy.

Controls, Quotas and Licenses: For the first almost three decades of planning (1951–80) in India, the prevailing regime used to be pejoratively called the 'license, quota, permit raj,' which summed up the chief feature of the system of physical controls that prevailed in the country. This characterisation also covertly conveyed the harmful socio-economic and political effects of the regime. Several black-operation effects of price and distribution controls, quotas and permits and industrial and import licenses will be discussed in the next chapter.

Deficiencies of the Tax System: For analytical clarity, I shall examine these deficiencies under two heads—high tax rates and a complex system of exemptions and deductions—and discuss them individually. I shall also restrict the discussion to only income tax, as other major taxes (excise duties and customs duties) will be discussed below separately.

High Personal Income Tax Rates: The discussion is generally limited to the brief period of three years in the early 1970s when the highest marginal income tax rate was pitched at the unbelievable ex-propriatory level of 97.75 per cent, though this rate had been generally very high during the entire 1960s. In addition, the rich were subjected to wealth tax.

It is generally agreed that tax evasion is dependent on the rates of taxation and rises with increase in the rates—that high rates make tax evasion much more attractive and profitable. For example, when the marginal rate of taxation is as high as 97.75 per cent, the net profit on concealment can be as much as 4400 per cent of (or 44 times) the after-tax income. In other words, at this marginal rate, it is more profitable at a certain level of income to evade tax on Rs 23 than to honestly earn Rs 1,000. In such a situation, it would be difficult for any person to resist the temptation to evade taxes.

From the foregoing, however, it does not necessarily follow that lowering the highest (and other top) marginal tax rate somewhat (from 97.75 per cent to, say, 80 per cent or even 70 per cent) will reduce tax evasion significantly. This is for at least two plausible reasons. One, even a marginal tax rate of 70 per cent may be considered too high by historical as well as international standards. Two, tax evasion, once practised, tends to persist even at lower marginal rates, unless the cost of evasion has become very high. This is because the tax evader, in his initiation of evasion, learns the ropes and soon gets used to the ways of evasion. Thereafter, it is not easy to wean him away from the practice of tax evasion merely by lowering the tax rates. However, a sizeable reduction in tax rates all along the progressive rate structure, with suitable simplifications, can be expected to have a wholesome effect on the tax response of the public as, at the margin, even the habitual tax evaders may not find it worth their while to indulge in the previous levels of evasion. Then, there are always new (or first-time) tax-payers who will decide about the extent of their tax evasion in the light of the prevailing tax rates and not very high marginal rates which prevailed for some time in the past.

Those who promise socialism (or at least containment of very high incomes) through a very high marginal income-tax rate on personal incomes, underrate grievously the propensities as well as powers of big tax-evaders and their collaborators, abettors and defenders in politics and the bureaucracy. But, policy-making is not heroics; nor should it be made a function of only one factor or goal to the utter neglect of other determining factors or governing conditions.

Exemptions and Deductions: I have already discussed in this section the problem of exemptions and deductions and the social cost thereof. This discussion also points to the abuse of these provisions for spurious tax avoidance, which is akin to tax evasion.

Inefficient and Corrupt Tax Administration: Other things beings the same, an efficient and honest tax administration is a positive asset to the economy and the government; but, an inadequate, inefficient and corrupt tax administration is an open invitation to all and sundry (and more particularly to habitual tax evaders) for tax evasion. Unfortunately, the tax administration in India is much closer to the second category than to the first.

Evasion of Excise Duties

Excise duties (ED) are duties or taxes on the domestic manufacture of commodities. They are divided between Union excise duties and state excise duties. The latter are limited mainly to the manufacture of liquor; practically all other excise duties come under Union excise. That is, they are levied and collected by the Union government, though their proceeds are shared with the state governments also. Thus, in the fiscal year 1988–89, the total receipts from Union EDs were Rs 18,441 crore, of which Rs 7,919 crore (more than 40 per cent) went to the states as their share and only Rs 10,992 crore went to the Union government. In gross terms, over the last three decades, EDs have been the single most important source of tax revenue to the government. Therefore, the health of the government budgets and, through them, of the economy, are affected greatly by ED realisation/evasion. For the Central government tax revenues alone, Union EDs are the second most important source of revenue, next only to customs duties.

In this section, I shall discuss the evasion of ED only. To conserve space, I shall not discuss the evasion of other indirect taxes, such as sales tax, which is the single most important source of indirect tax revenue to the state governments, or state ED. However, while guesstimating black income in Chapter 5, I shall take full note of their evasion, too.

The evasion of ED leads to the evasion of several other taxes, namely, sales tax, corporation tax, personal income tax and wealth tax. This can be easily explained. ED evasion (whether through the suppression of output or undervaluation or misclassification or other means) implies that a part of the true (market) value of output is not shown in the books of the producer, and thus escapes a part of the sales tax due. The undeclared output is sold without any *pucca* (regular) invoice and challan. If this output is used as an input (intermediate goods) in the manufacture of other excisable items, it both facilitates and compels the non-declaration of the latter manufacture for tax purposes. If the output is of final goods subject to sales tax, this output is also sold clandestinely without the seller (trader) paying the sales tax due. Corporation tax gets evaded because, with a view to lower one's excise duty liability, total output (or clearances) for specific duties and the value of this output for *ad valorem* duty are understated, without any corresponding reduction in corporate expenses. Thereby, the net taxable profits are understated and a part of the corporate tax due is evaded. The chief beneficiaries of this kind of evasion are not the shareholders (as dividends are distributed only out of the accounted profits), but the members of the controlling group and top management who (mis)appropriate the sums involved in a variety of ways. To the extent corporate profits are understated, given the normal pay-out ratio, the dividend income of shareholders is also lower than otherwise and so their personal income tax liability is also lower. Given the progressive rate structure and the fact that the bulk of dividend income accrues to the high income-tax-payers, the loss of revenue from the derived evasion of personal income tax is also relatively high. This argument applies equally forcefully to producers organised under non-corporate forms, namely, private limited companies, partnerships and single entrepreneurships. It is these forms which abound in the small industry sector, and to a point in even medium-scale industry. Our argument can be easily extended to the evasion of wealth tax also, as assets accumulated through savings of black income generally remain undeclared or grossly undervalued or understated.

Till 1975, excises were selective in coverage. In that year, a new residuary Tariff Item No. 68 was introduced, whereby all domestically manufactured goods not specified elsewhere were brought under the purview of ED. Thereby, the excise coverage became near universal, with allowance for various exemptions. In the budget for 1986–87, the Tariff Item No. 68 was abolished and all the goods falling under this item were distributed under appropriate heads under a new system of classification adopted in that year. The new system adopted is designed to be comprehensive in product coverage and its commodity classification is supposed to be in harmony with market usage as well as customs' classification. It is supposed to minimise 'classification disputes' about the correct tariff category of a particular product.

Commodity-group-wise excise revenue yield varies a good deal across the board. Traditionally, three commodity groups—namely, petroleum products, textiles (mainly manmade fibres, yarn and fabrics) and cigarettes—have been the most important revenue-earners. Together, they contribute about 44 per cent of the total excise revenue. Other important earners of excise revenue are cement, iron and steel products, tyres, sugar and motor vehicles.

ED evasion in India is both widespread and large. This is supported by official enquiries, such as of the Venkatappiah Committee (1973) as well as independent research studies such as of Rao (1979), Khadye (1981) and Sury (1985). Reference may also be made to the studies of the Jha Committee (1978), Dandekar Committee (1980), Jain (1983), Rao and Pradhan (1985), Sinha (1983), Kumar (1985), Misra Study Group (1985) and Ninan (1985).

On ED evasion, the Venkatappiah Committee (1973) had observed that 'evasion of duty is considerable and, in certain sectors, pervasive'. The statement continues to sum up well the state of affairs in respect to ED evasion today. It may be added that the Committee's conclusion was based on the mass of information collected by it, that is, on the totality of what they had seen, heard and investigated. The Committee had admitted that they were 'painfully surprised at the range, diversity and, in certain segments of production, almost the universality of the evasion which is practised by those who produce the goods' (1973: 55).

Speaking of integrated tax evasion, (involving the evasion of excise duty, sales tax, income tax, and so on), the Committee had made a highly insightful and pertinent statement when it said that

> *evasion of taxes . . . has become a way of life* with significant sections of industry and trade . . . a way of life which has been gaining ground in the country over many years; it is a way of life that is not confined to any one class of people, but is based on the spreading conviction that money is the key and black money the master key to power and influence (1973: 54, emphasis added).

Unforutnately, the situation today is much worse than better.

The most common *methods of ED-evasion* are discussed briefly below.

Suppression of Production: Suppression of production is known to be very common in small-scale industries (such as electrical goods, steel furniture and utensils, khandsari, plastics and art silk fabrics). It is generally underreported in medium-scale and large-scale industries. Common methods employed are the following:

(*a*) Raw materials are not fully accounted for, especially when a close relationship exists between the raw materials and finished products. The producers get away with duty evasion by buying a part of the raw materials in black, or claiming extra wastage in production.

(*b*) Statutory records are not kept up-to-date to enable the manufacturer to make last-minute manipulations.

(*c*) Gate passes are issued without indicating the time and date of removal of goods from the factory, to facilitate the use of the same gate pass for duplicate transportation, particularly when the movement involved is within the same town or city.

(*d*) Duty-paid depots are kept in areas adjacent to the place of manufacture. This makes it easier for the manufacturer to remove goods clandestinely to these depots and claim that these goods are already duty-paid. Movement of goods from these depots does not require any gate pass.

Undervaluation: This is the most important method of duty evasion, particularly in the organised sector and in respect to *ad valorem* duties. For undervaluation, several methods are used:

(*a*) Under-invoicing the product and taking the balance of the under-valued amount under the table.

(*b*) Reducing the sale price of the product to the dealer and, at the same time, maintaining the retail price of the product, thereby increasing the dealer's margin of profit. This is truly fictitious because, in return, the dealer is required to incur certain expenditures which are statutorily the responsibility of the manufacturer (like compulsory after-sales service under the product warranty) or passing on to the dealer certain post-manufacturing expenses on publicity, sales promotion, and so on. If the dealer does not incur the stipulated expenditures, the manufacturer raises debit notes against the dealer.

(*c*) Another method of undervaluation is to show certain expenses as technical expenses. Invoices for them are raised by the headquarters office, whereas output invoices are raised from the factory, which alone involves excise duty.

(*d*) Floating of *benami* (bogus) agencies, which either raise supplementary invoices and/or collect the differential in value from dealers. At times, they may also be used to sell a large part (say 80 per cent) of the output at a higher than the declared price, and only a small balance of the output at the factory gate at a lower declared price to favoured clients and to those who buy the bulk of their supplies through the bogus agency at the higher effective price.

(*e*) Invoices are manipulated to show a certain portion of manufacturing expenses as post-manufacturing expenses (such as transport costs), which are not includible in the assessable value.

Misclassification of Goods: In several cases, the tariff provides numerous classifications and sub-classifications, carrying different rates of duty, depending on such factors as chemical composition, blend, thickness, fineness, count and denierage. In some cases, the spread among the differential rates of duty for different subcategories of the same tariff item or of allied products in different items is very large. The tariff on cotton and manmade yarn and fabrics, paper, paints and varnishes, plastics and chemicals are said to be classic examples in which it is very easy as well as common for the producer to misclassify his goods with a view to minimising his duty liability.

In certain cases, this practice even takes the form of 'misdeclaration' of goods, which should be distinguished from simple misclassification of goods, discussed in the foregoing. Under misdeclaration, 'high-duty excisable' goods (such as compressors) are billed as non-taxable items (for instance, as accessories) and the difference in the market values of two kinds of items is recovered in black. In the textile industry, it is not uncommon to declare and get cleared sound fabrics as fents and rags.

Misuse of Exemptions: Exemptions of various sorts run through the whole excise system in India. Their misuse, especially by the small-scale industry units, is also believed to be widespread. Exemptions, after all, are contingent on a wide variety of conditions, such as the value of the goods produced by a manufacturer, the end use of a product, its exports, the use of power, the raw materials used in the manufacture of a product, and the composition of a finished product. Each of these conditions has been misused by industry (more so, by the small-scale industry) to evade duty as far as possible.

Excise Disputes: In recent years, excise disputes have become an increasingly important method of tax evasion, as a large proportion of these disputes are *fabricated disputes*. Most of the time, apart from attempted duty evasion, the motive is to gain interest-free use of funds for the period of the dispute and also to earn fortuitous gain. The former gain arises because interest is not chargeable on disputed duty arrears. The latter gain arises because the manufacturers mostly do charge duty from customers, but not pay it to the government or claim its refund, if paid. These gains accrue to recalcitrant assessees, because the settlement of all disputes tends to be long-drawn. The device most often used is to procure interim court stays, which are then contrived to remain in force for long periods.

As a result of mounting excise disputes, government claims of duty evasion have also been rising rapidly. For example, these claims, which had stood at a mere Rs 70 crore in 1984, rose to almost Rs 5,000 crore by the end of 1988. Of this, the claim against the cigarette giant, ITC (Indian Tobacco Co.), alone was Rs 1,100 crore.

Most excise disputes have traditionally been classification and valuation disputes. But, in recent years, in value terms, the disputes regarding post-manufacturing expenses (PME), such as advertising, packing and freight costs, have become most important. It is claimed by the companies that, as ruled by the Supreme Court also, these costs are not assessable to duty, as ED is leviable only on manufacturing costs. This much is generally accepted. The official case, however, is that companies are inflating expenses on these items so as to reduce ED liability. For example, cigarette companies, which once had PME as low as 1 per cent of the manufacturing cost, are reported to have claimed PME as high as 20 per cent of the manufacturing cost. Then, there are also disputes about the misclassification of products, about fictitious trade discounts that are recovered from dealers, about charging ED from customers without having paid it to the government, and so on.

Thus, there is a regular tug-of-war that has been going on between the government and the cigarette companies, in which the latter have always tried to beat the excise law till the government plugged the loophole. With EDs more than 300 per cent of the assessable value, the temptation to evade it is truly very high. It is generally held that rapid expansions and diversifications by cigarette companies have been financed by tax-evaded cigarette money. The same money is also recycled back into the cigarette business by financing purchases of inputs with it.

Factors Reponsible for ED Evasion

The factors responsible for ED evasion are many. They are discussed briefly below.

Political Corruption

All sorts of tax evasion and other black operations are encouraged or abetted in a general climate of political corruption, as the tax-evaders and black operators know they can buy their clearance or acquittal with bribes to persons in authority and contributions to party funds. I have already discussed this factor in Chapter 2.

Besides this general factor, there are ED-specific factors that arise from the special features of the ED system of India. This is explained below.

Multiplicity and the Wide Range of ED Rates

We should first recognise the distinction between the statutory (or tariff) rate and the effective rate. The statutory rate on each commodity is the maximum leviable rate passed by Parliament and incorporated in the Tariff Schedule. The government, by itself, has no power to enhance these rates. But, within the span of these tariff rates, it fixes and alters the rates of duties known as 'effective rates' by the issue of notifications under the power delegated to it by Parliament. It is also vested with powers to exempt, by issue of notifications, any excisable product either wholly or partially from the ED leviable on it. The exemption may be either general and unconditional, or specific and subject to certain conditions. Consequently, the effective ED structure is highly complex due to a large number of rates within a single Tariff Item, enforced by several notifications, changes made in it in an *ad hoc* and haphazard manner from time to time, and the operation of hundreds of exemption schemes. The effective rates at any time could be easily more than two thousand. In the early 1970s, there were more than 300 effective rates as against 17 tariff rates for cotton fabrics alone. In 1987–88, there were more than 10,000 commodities bearing separate mention and duty rate in the duty manual based on product differentiation connected with different sizes and shapes. Effective rates also have a very *wide range*, extending from 2 per cent to over 400 per cent. This, coupled with the complexity of the ED structure, has induced as well as facilitated much ED evasion and avoidance and offered much scope for bureaucratic discretion as well as corruption through several methods discussed later in this section.

Exemptions

Exemptions are another very important feature of the present excise system. They pervade the whole tariff. They are used to refine the description of excisable goods by dividing them into categories and sub-categories, and separate rates of duty are prescribed for each of these along with appropriate conditions, criteria and safeguards. They are used as a versatile tool for the realisation of a large number of social and economic objectives. The pervasive use of exemptions is pointed out by the fact that, at the end of March 1985, as many as 533 exemption notifications of basic duties of excise were extant. With so many exemptions around, the ED system has become highly complex and full of ambiguities as well as loopholes, which are utilised fruitfully by ED-evaders. This tends to invite much pressure from industry for 'tailor-made' rates to suit particular firms. Thereby, such firms have gained extra crores of rupees annually in comparison with competing firms. This avenue promotes political and bureaucratic corruption, causes distortions in industry and unhealthy competition among manufacturers.

Specific Duties

Another feature of India's ED system is the preponderance of specific duties—duties per unit of output—in comparison with *ad valorem* duties, that is, duties that are stipulated as a certain percentage of the value of output. It is well-known that specific duties suffer from the defect that their revenue yields do not keep pace with inflation, and so they lack built-in flexibility or an automatic revenue raising capacity with inflation. The opposite is the case with *ad valorem* duties. Yet, specific duties predominate in India largely because of difficulties in administering *ad valorem* levies, the large volume of litigation and the risk of avoidance or evasion through manipulation of assessable value.

Taxation of Inputs

The taxation of inputs leads to the 'cascading' (duty upon duty) of taxes when an input passes through various stages of manufacturing in the form of marketable commodities, and is assessed for duty at each stage. This makes the ED burden on downstream producers much heavier than if direct ED was levied on their produce, increases their costs and reduces their competitiveness in the market. The tax relief offered in the form of 'proforma credit' and MODVAT is highly inadequate. Therefore, the downstream producers are pushed into evading ED.

Assessment Procedures

These procedures play an important role in inducing excise disputes avoidance and evasion of duty and so affect revenue realisation For the first twenty-four years of ED life (1944–68), a system of physical control of the manufacturing of all excised commodities prevailed, under which close checks and supervision were exercised over the production, packing, storage and clearance of such goods. They were allowed to be cleared only on the prepayment of duty. In December 1949, the current system of 'gate pass' was introduced. Such a pass authenticated all the pertinent information about the goods to be cleared and the amount of ED paid. Only on its production were goods allowed to be moved out of the factory. Because of its irksome features, the physical control system attracted a lot of criticism from manufacturers on the grounds of excessive interference and harassment by the excise department field staff, their all-round corruption and high costs of compliance.

So, in 1968–69, a new assessment procedure, known as the 'self-removal procedure' (SRP) was adopted. With minor changes, it has continued ever since. Under it, every producer of excisable goods is required to submit to the excise officer concerned, for his approval, a *classification list* of the goods produced or warehoused by him and, in the case of goods with *ad valorem* duty, a *price list*, showing the price of each such good and discounts, if any, allowed to the buyers. After the approval of these lists, the duty liability of goods intended to be cleared is determined by the producer himself. He is permitted to clear them on a gate pass, not required to be countersigned by a central excise officer, at any time and on any day (except the Budget day when standard physical control provisions apply). The facility for provisional assessment of goods in cases of disputes or delay exists. A separate current account has to be maintained with the Department for each commodity.

Under the SRP, ED evasion in general has gone up as, in the absence of checks of the 'physical control procedure,' it has been much easier for the manufacturers to evade ED.

Duty Concessions to Small-Scale Industry (SSI) Units

This has been a salient feature of India's ED system. These concessions have been universally misused for duty evasion. A large part of this duty concession and evasion is availed of by large companies through small ancillary units set up by them and/or through marketing arrangements for the produce of SSI units.

The foregoing discussion suggests that to reduce ED evasion drastically, it is necessary to simplify and rationalise the present ED system, for instance, by cutting down drastically the number of effective duty rates as well as exemptions and the greater use of computerisation. Of course, this must be fully supported by a vast improvement in the general climate of corruption.

Evasion of Customs Duties

Since I have already discussed various relevant aspects of the evasion of excise duties in the previous section, and since the methods of customs-duty evasion and the factors responsible for such evasion are broadly similar to those discussed in the foregoing, I shall be relatively brief in my discussion of the evasion of customs duties here. Also, much less well-documented information is available on customs-duty evasion than on excise-duty evasion.

Formally, customs duties are duties (taxes) on the flow of goods traded across the borders of a country—that is, on the import of goods into India from other countries as well as the export of goods out of India. But, as most of these exports are duty free and others are subject to a very low rate of duty, for all practical purposes, customs duty in India stands for only import duties.

After Union excise duties, customs duties are the second largest source of revenue to the government. For example, in 1988–89, in the total tax revenue of Rs 44,419 crore collected by the Central government (inclusive of the states' share of personal income tax and Union excise duties), customs duties contributed Rs 15,805 crore (or 35.6 per cent), whereas Union excise duties contributed Rs 18,841 crore (or 42.4 per cent) of the total tax revenue.

Customs duties are levied and collected by the Central government. Its revenues are retained fully by it and not shared with the state governments. Customs duties, generally, are *ad valorem* duties. They are levied on practically all goods imported into India, except foodgrains, which are imported duty-free on government account only. In special cases, the government does allow the duty-free import of goods. Additionally, under the 'baggage rules,' Indians returning to India after spending some time abroad are granted a certain duty-free baggage allowance. Import duties, besides yielding a sizable amount of revenue to the government, protect domestic industries against foreign competition. It is now generally held that the resulting protection to the industry has been a mixed blessing—whereas it has fostered domestic industry and encouraged much import substitution, it has also made Indian industry least quality- and cost-conscious, and neither innovative nor self-confident and ready to face fair foreign competition.

The general level of duty rates in India has been very high, with an average duty rate of more than 80 per cent *ad valorem* on non-food imports. The overall range of these duties is also very high—with a low of 40 per cent and a high of 450 per cent. The import of most electronic goods (like VCRs) and synthetic fabrics has been subject to duty rates of 250 per cent *ad valorem* or more. High duty rates and import licensing serve as potent inducements for the evasion of such duties (through underinvoicing) and for smuggling. Too much diversity in the rates of duty on commodities covered by a particular tariff item also offers much scope for duty evasion through the misclassification/misdeclaration of goods imported. As a result, the realised (also called 'effective') rate of duty on non-food imports was only 26.3 per cent in 1980–81, 34.7 per cent in 1983–84 and 62.0 per cent in 1987–88.

As in the case of excise-duty evasion, several methods of customs-duty evasion are used. The most important ones are discussed briefly below.

Undervaluation

Undervaluation is accomplished through the *under-invoicing* of imports, by arrangement with the foreign supplier of goods who, in most cases, willingly obliges the Indian importer with a lower-value invoice, provided the Indian importer pays in foreign currency the full difference between the actual price and the lower invoiced price of the goods imported. The foreign supplier also gains from this black transaction, because his accounted profits and tax liability (in his country) also go down. For the Indian importer, however, the under-invoicing of imports requires that the importer buys the required amount of foreign exchange (to pay in full the actual price of imports) in the black market at a premium. This is an additional cost for this black transaction. It reduces the net profit of the importer through under-invoicing. The net profit now is given by the excess of the tariff rate over the foreign-exchange premium rate (per rupee of undervaluation). I shall discuss the manipulation of invoicing (for imports as well as exports and under- as well as over-invoicing) more fully in the next section in the context of 'foreign exchange leakages'.

The deterrence or promotion of the aforesaid undervaluation is greatly affected by the altertness and uprightness of the customs staff. Their technical competence can be improved through proper selection and training. There are no easy ways to improve personal honesty. Yet, proper checks and balances can be helpful. Currently, the customs staff does carry with it price information about the major articles of import from the better-known suppliers and the general rates of discount, so that in such cases under-invoicing can be easily detected.

Misclassification/Misdeclaration of Goods

To reduce the duty burden, false declarations about goods imported in the documents (such as bills of lading) submitted to the customs are made and higher-duty goods are cleared on payment of lower duty charged on the misdeclared goods. Much, however, depends on the efficiency, vigilance and integrity of the customs staff. If the staff is efficient, well-trained, vigilant and honest, such malpractices will be discouraged and reduced. But, if they can be easily bribed and are not alive and honest to their duties and responsibilities or succumb easily to 'outside' pressures, including political pressure, the outcomes are otherwise. Several cases of fraudulent declarations get reported in the press. (No such documentation by the customs is available.) For example, it has been common to import sound woollen fabrics and even suits in the name of rags. The import of duty-free fodder machines, which had attracted a lot of public attention during 1989, is another similar example.

Smuggling

This will be discussed at length in the next chapter.

Trade Controls and Foreign Exchange Leakages

Foreign trade has been another important area for earning large amounts of black income. I shall study this aspect in relation to import controls and licenses and export controls and export promotion. Besides, I shall also examine foreign exchange leakages, the black market in foreign exchange, *hawala* transations in foreign exchange, and the moves towards trade liberalisation since March 1985.

Import (Trade) Control

Import control was first introduced in India in May 1940 to conserve and regulate the use of scarce foreign exchange and available shipping space for the war effort and for essential civilian supplies. The import licensing system had its origin in the Imports and Exports (Control) Act of 1947. In 1955, a comprehensive Import Trade Control Order was issued, which brought almost all imports under the purview of licensing. Despite several relaxations and liberalisations since the mid-1980s, the basic framework of the import trade control system remained more or less intact till the middle of 1991, when a beginning was made towards liberalising India's foreign trade and moving it away from a system of administrative controls and licenses. I shall study briefly the attempts towards trade liberalisation later in the chapter.

Under the old policy regime (for a detailed discussion, see Bhagwati and Desai, 1970, Ch. 15), the most noticeable form of import control was the direct rationing of scarce foreign exchange by the government through the issue of import licenses to intending importers. An import license authorised the licensee to import specific goods up to a particular value specified in the license. There were more than a dozen types of licenses, with their further sub-categories. Each type of license was governed by its own procedure and carried its own list of commodities. For example, there were items which were on Open General License or OGL (with or without the 'actual user' condition), restricted items, banned items, items subject to export-import links, items which were subject to quota for 'established importers,' and items whose imports were linked to a specific user industry. In the absence of an effective monitoring system (and with large-scale foreign exchange leakages and smuggling), this kind of highly differentiated import licensing system with item-wise restrictions had not served its basic objective of restricting the import of any particular product to the desired degree. Further, much office personnel time was spent on the revalidation/amendment of past AU (actual user) licenses and less on promotional and other activities.

Under the import licensing system, foreign exchange utilisation was exercised through administrative decisions over the allocation of foreign exchange for practically all uses in the economy—trade and travel, amongst others. This was done not only by industries, but also by firms and plants. Different administrative agencies (such as the Directorate General of Technical Development, DGTD, and the Iron and Steel Controller) were involved in dividing up the bulk allocation among units. Otherwise, most of the import licenses were issued by the Chief Controller of Imports and Exports. In the licensing procedure, two major criteria were used: the principle of 'essentiality' certified by the sponsoring government agency, and the principle of 'indigenous non-availability' of the good(s) to be imported, attested by a 'clearing agency'. Apart from these, no priorities were worked out and no clear and rational basis were used for industry-wise allocation, as the number of industries was much too large. As a consequence, some rule of thumb (such as pro rata allocation with reference to installed capacity or employment or past imports) had been used. The allocations among units were *ad hoc* and discretionary.

A regular feature of the regime of import trade and foreign exchange controls was black market in imports and import licenses. This was also an important source of black income generation. According to the Santhanam Committee (1964: 18), in the early 1960s, the black market premia on import licenses varied between 100 per cent and 500 per cent of the licensed value. Such premia have had several deleterious effects. First, they (along with high import tariffs) have induced several kinds of illegal activities, such as the generation and use of unauthorised foreign exchange (through the faking of invoices) and smuggling. Second, the black market premia have encouraged several malpractices in the scramble for import licences. For example, unscruplous operators have claimed these licenses on the basis of false or forged 'essentiality certificates' from the Director of Industries (obtained by misrepresentation) and false indigenous nonavailability certificates, false or forged records of past imports, false turnover certificates from chartered accountants, and false income-tax clearance certificates (see Bhagwati and Desai, 1970: 308–9). At times, even the licenses themselves were forged or tampered with or issued in the name of bogus (non-existing) firms. Third, in the awarding of licenses, much corruption and favourtism were indulged in by bureaucrats and politicians. Further, the methods used for extorting bribes from the applicants for licenses had their own unwholesome effects on the public morale and production efficiency and involved much harassment and avoidable wastage of time and energy. Fourth, there was much illegal traffic in import licenses. In fact, bogus firms used to 'go into business' to obtain import licenses and resell them to other firms at a premium. Alternatively, imports were sold in black. For the various reasons indicated in the foregoing, large firms with their large resources and better contacts with the high-ups in the bureaucracy and politics have generally been able to appropriate a very large proportion of the total licensed import value. Fifth, high premia or unearned surplus, or what economists call 'rent' had been attracting the country's real resources into purely rent-seeking activities, with high welfare costs (see, for instance, Krueger, 1974). In Appendix A of this book, I have evaluated the Krueger-type analysis, interpreted as a (generalised) theory of black income.

Export Controls

Export controls have taken two main forms: pre-export inspection of goods and control over export receipts. Pre-export inspection of goods ensure quality control and that the goods actually being exported are as per declaration in the shipping documents. It is generally held that there is much need and ample scope for improvement in each of these directions to discourage frauds of various kinds. For example, misdeclaration/misclassification of exports may be attempted in order to claim REP licenses for higher value, though unrelated, imports. At times, only waste or low-value goods are exported in place of the declared exports. Misdeclaration may also be attempted in order to reduce the export-duty liability. This happens when, for example, viscose and nylon fabrics with higher export duty are passed off as silk fabric with no or lower export duty.

Control over export receipts is a very important part of exchange control. Its purpose is to ensure that export earnings are brought into the country and sold to the RBI, the sole controller of all foreign exchange in the country.

The instrument of control is mainly the GR [that is, Goods (Revised)] form. While making the shipment, every exporter is required to fill up the GR form in triplicate, which is then handed over to the customs authorities. The customs verify the details, particularly the basis of valuation and the value of exports, and record their valuation on all three copies. The original is sent to the RBI and the other two copies are returned to the exporter after entering a 'security number' for easy identification. The exporter submits the shipping documents with the invoice and other documents (including the duplicate and triplicate copies of the GR form) to a bank. The bank then realises the value of the exports on behalf of its client. The bank in question forwards the duplicate form to the RBI immediately and the triplicate after full realisation.

The Dagli Committee (1979: 96–97) has brought to note the following features of the above procedure:

1. The RBI has no role to play in checking whether the exporter has declared the full value of exports. That is, leakages through the under-invoicing of exports cannot be checked by the RBI. Some GR form duplicates and triplicates may not be submitted to a bank at all. This makes for the retention abroad of export earnings illegally.
2. There is considerable physical movement of GR forms from the customs to the RBI, from the exporters' banks to the RBI, and queries from the RBI to the exporters through their banks. In this movement, some forms always get lost.
3. Considering the very large number of GR forms involved—12 lakh were received by the RBI in 1975–76 only—the physical transport and checking of so much paper is cumbersome and wasteful. With the increase in the volume and diversification of exports, the increase in the volume of paper is becoming more unmanageable.

Maluse of Export-Promotion Schemes: Several kinds of maluses and frauds associated with the operation of these schemes have come to light (see, for instance, Dhar, 1990). They have caused much illegal drain of hard currency foreign exchange as well as loss of revenue to the government. For the year 1989–90 alone, this loss was put at about Rs 1,000 crore.

This maluse has taken various forms. The major ones are given below:

1. I shall discuss later in this section, the device of misclassification/misdeclaration of exports to gain undeservedly higher value import entitlements and to lower export-duty liability.
2. Most importantly, the Duty Exemption Entitlement Certificate (DEEC) Scheme 'under advance licensing' has been put to much misuse. The scheme allows a firm to import raw materials and components free of duty, provided they are used in goods meant for exports. It is reported that, under the scheme, non-existent DEEC-holders obtain advance licenses for imports by furnishing fictitious information provided by chartered accountants and chartered engineers. Then, the goods so imported by DEEC holders are sold by them in the domestic market at hefty premia, whereas cheaper locally-produced materials are used instead in the export products. It was further reported that, under the scheme, import duty worth nearly Rs 1,500 crore was exempted in 1988 and Rs 2,000 crore in 1989. In the opinion of customs officials, at least 30–40 per cent of these amounts should not have been exempted. Since it was introduced along with advance licensing in 1978, over time, several changes have been introduced in the scheme. The rules governing the scheme have been made very complex. The law suffers from several loopholes. Lax enforcement further helps leakages under the scheme.
3. Cases of large-scale malpractices by some 100 per cent export-oriented units (in the form of selling off duty-free imported material and taking out manufactured goods for sale in the domestic market without authority) have also come to light. There have also been several cases of overvaluation of exports and of fictitious exports, with the avowed

purpose of claiming higher incentives in the form of CCS, duty drawbacks and higher REP licenses for imports. Another kind of fraud practised in export trade is represented by the practice of 'switch trade'. Under it, goods declared as exports to some rupee-trade country (say, in eastern Europe) are diverted on the way to a hard-currency country with a view to earn more valuable foreign exchange, which is not repatriated officially to the country.

Foreign Exchange Leakages

Foreign exchange leakages are a necessary accompaniment of high import tariffs and comprehensive foreign exchange control. Conditions of foreign exchange shortage over most of the last half a century, coupled with the policy of planned utilisation of this scarce resource (especially since the beginning of the Second Five Year Plan in 1956) have necessitated the continuation and further strengthening of the foreign exchange control first instituted in 1939. This has also given birth to the emergence of a black market in foreign exchange, where foreign currency is bought and sold at an exchange rate determined by the forces of demand and supply. This black market exchange rate is always above the official exchange rate, when expressed as the price of foreign currency (say, the US dollar) in terms of Indian rupees. That is, foreign exchange is sold at a premium, which may be expressed as a percentage of the official exchange rate (in rupees). As we shall see later, the premium rate itself is determined by the joint forces of demand and supply in black market for foreign exchange and, in turn, negatively affects the demand for foreign exchange and positively affects the supply of it in this market.

Therefore, foreign exchange leakages are best discussed in the framework of the demand for and the supply of foreign exchange in black. I shall start with an analysis of the sources of the supply of black foreign exchange or of the leakages of foreign exchange. The two sources are the same, except that the supply is also affected by the hoarding/releases of black foreign exchange accumulated in foreign countries by resident Indians, in addition to the current leakages of foreign exchange. With this difference in mind, I shall discuss below the main sources of foreign exchange leakages. (See also Kaul Committee, 1971.)

The main sources of foreign exchange leakages are:

1. Manipulations through trade channels:
   (*a*) under-invoicing of exports,
   (*b*) over-invoicing of imports,
   (*c*) other trade-related leakages;
2. Inward remittances of foreign exchange through illegal channels;
3. Smuggling of goods out of India, such as silver, animal skins, antiques, and narcotics; and
4. Illegal purchase of foreign exchange from foreign tourists and others visiting India.

I shall discuss below each of these sources.

Under-invoicing of Exports: Under-invoicing of exports involves under-declaration of the true value of exports as, under the exchange control requirement of the country, an exporter is required to bring into the country only the declared value of exports. He can receive the remaining (undeclared) part of the value of exports in the form, manner and place of his choice. Thus, through this simple device, an exporter gains free foreign exchange, which he can use freely in any way he likes.

A person who is in the business of both import and export may under-invoice his exports to enable him to under-invoice his imports too, and thereby evade a part of high import duty. In this double operation, the foreign exchange generated by under-invoicing of exports is used to meet the differential between the correct value and the under-invoiced value of the imported goods.

More importantly and essentially, the inducement to generate illegal foreign exchange (through whatever methods open to individuals and firms) is the prospect of net earning from it. Ordinarily, this is given by the black market premium rate on foreign exchange which can be realised through its sale in black minus, of course, the risk premium rate to compensate for risks undertaken in illegal transactions (namely, faking of invoices and the sale of foreign exchange in the black market). In the case of under-invoicing of exports in India, however, there is a complication presented by the presence of export 'subsidies' in various forms, which have been given in India since 1962 on the *net fob* export value. These subsidies act as the opportunity cost of earning a black-market premium on black foreign exchange generated through the under-invoicing of exports. In any case of under-invoicing of exports, the net profit is given by the total of black-market premium (on free foreign exchange realised), net of risk premium minus its total opportunity cost given by the net of tax export subsidies foregone.

Symbolically, the incentive to under-invoice exports will exist when $p > s + \pi$, where

> p = black market premium rate on foreign exchange (say, per US dollar),
> s = *ad valorem* subsidy rate per dollar worth of exports, and
> π = risk premium rate per dollar worth of invoice faking and black market sale of foreign exchange.

(The formula given above can be suitably adapted in other cases of invoice manipulation involving over-invoicing of exports or of imports or under-invoicing of imports.)

Five points about the high vulnerability of certain export commodities may be noted.

First, high undervaluation is usually suspected in the case of jute manufactures. This undervaluation is facilitated by the fact that exporters have their overseas associates—mills having their own export houses or export/shipping departments; some associates are either subsidiaries or principals of Indian exporters, some are agents and some others are independent business houses which have a long-standing business relationship with the Indian exporters. These overseas associates register a forward delivery contract when the ruling price is low, without declaring the higher realised price or substituting the earlier registered contract at the higher price by another contract for the ruling lower price. Undervaluation also takes place through the misdeclaration of production, yardage or weight.

Similarly, in recent years, large exporters of gems have also organised their own sister concerns in major export markets (Belgium and the US) to facilitate under-invoicing of their exports.

Second, most of the tea sold through auctions, which is shipped to London on a consignment (sale) basis to parties abroad who have some financial link or some other interest with the Indian exporter, offers much scope for under-invoicing. Further, variations in the quality of tea are not easily identifiable by physical examination.

Third, the export of metal ores (for instance, iron ore or manganese ore), concentrates and metal scrap offers much scope for the leakage of foreign exchange through the manipulation of analysis results, for example, of iron or manganese content, or weighment, or through the operation of despatch/demurrage clauses of agreements, or through freight manipulations.

Fourth, invoice manipulation through the misdeclaration of quality (because of non-standardisation) is fairly common in the case of items such as hides, skins, leather, unmanufactured tobacco, groundnut oil cakes, marine products, spices, mica, diamonds and other precious stones.

Fifth, since a valuation check is difficult in the case of engineering goods, they offer high scope for invoice manipulation, though compensating advantages in the form of several export 'subsidies' militate against it.

Over-Invoicing of Imports: The scope for over-invoicing imports has been rather limited. This is largely because of the heavy import tariff structure so that, in most cases, the possible gain of foreign exchange through the over-invoicing of imports (and the black-market premium of foreign exchange) is more than washed off by the extra cost of import duty and the premium for risk involved in the illegal activities of over-invoicing and the sale of foreign exchange in the black market. Yet there are also commodities with relatively low rates of import duty as, for example, capital equipment and machinery. They offer much scope for over-invoicing as the valuation of capital equipment and custom-built machinery is a difficult task. Further, the commodities under OGL and duty-free license are also susceptible to over-invoicing of imports. Examples are hides and skins, raw cashew and books, among others.

Invoice manipulation in the opposite direction, that is, the under-invoicing of imports and the over-invoicing of exports, also takes place in actual practice. This creates a demand for unauthorised foreign exchange. *Prima facie*, it appears as though the country does not suffer any loss of foreign exchange when some imports are under-invoiced. But, in reality, to the extent some imports are under-invoiced, foreign exchange has to be found by the importer from unauthorised channels to pay the differential to the foreign exporter between the correct import value and the under-invoiced value. This adds to pressures for generating unauthorised foreign exchange. Besides, there is a loss of customs duty, as no duty is chargeable on the value suppressed.

The over-invoicing of exports also does not result in greater foreign exchange earning, as would superficially appear to be the position. This is because, in such cases, either the exporter does not repatriate the over-invoiced value or buys the required foreign exchange (to be paid to the RBI) in black to make up for the differential between the over-invoiced value of goods exported and their correct value.

A number of cases of over-invoicing of exports occurred prior to the devaluation of the rupee in June 1966, when certain export-promotion schemes (especially the import entitlement schemes) were in force and the black market premium on import licenses was very high—mostly more than 100 per cent of the licensed value of imports. Under these schemes, import licenses related to the net *fob* value of exports were granted liberally to exporters even before the actual repatriation of the sale proceeds of exports. Some parties obtained import licenses on the basis of the over-invoiced value of exports, but subsequently failed to repatriate the over-invoiced amount.

Apart from the scope for the above-mentioned two kinds of invoice manipulation, the condition of net profitability from such manipulations should also be satisfied for them to be undertaken by the traders. That is, imports will be under-invoiced only if the gain from the lower import duty burden exceeds the premium cost of foreign exchange to be purchased in black and the premium for risk involved in such a venture. Similarly, over-invoicing of exports will be induced only if the gain from additional subsidy exceeds the cost thereof given by the premium cost of foreign exchange purchased in black and the premium for risk involved in the act of over-invoicing and the black market puchase of foreign exchange.

Other Trade-Related Leakages: A complete enumeration of other trade-related leakages will not be made here. Instead, only two examples of malpractices are given below.

In the case of imports, while the value declared may be correct for the goods as shown in the documents, fraud may be perpetrated by bringing in worthless goods under those documents. Thereby the bulk of foreign exchange (after deducting the foreign cost of these worthless goods and the cost of packing, forwarding, shipping, and so on) is misappropriated by the importer. In such cases, even advance remittance of funds may be secured and, to avoid easy detection, the delivery of goods is not taken. Imports against forged licenses and remittances against forged bills of lading are other known malpractices.

On the export side, at times, exports are made under fictitious names or the GR forms (evidencing exports) may be lost. This makes it impossible to ensure the repatriation of the sale proceeds.

Other Sources of Foreign Exchange Leakages: Of the other sources of foreign exchange leakages, I shall discuss the 'smuggling out of goods from India' in the next chapter; the other two sources are discussed very briefly below.

First, let us consider inward remittances of funds from Indians residing abroad (as, for example, in the oil-rich Gulf countries, USA, Canada, and UK). Such remittances have become a rich source of foreign exchange to India, especially after the oil crisis of 1973. These funds are basically support funds for the dependents of Indians working abroad. Obviously, these recorded annual flows represent the funds in foreign currency sent to India through official banking channels. Besides these, there are also illegal channels through which these flows are remitted. It is the latter remittances which serve as a leakage. How big this leakage is cannot be easily estimated. But, in knowledgeable circles, it is considered to be quite large.

The second source is the illegal purchase of foreign exchange from foreign tourists and other visitors. Some foreign exchange also leaks out when foreign tourists and others visiting India sell their foreign currency in exchange for rupees to private parties. Usually this is done to gain more than the official exchange rate. Knowing this, agents of specialist firms, their touts and other private individuals regularly frequent places of tourist interest, hotels, and so on, to make their purchases of foreign currency. Again, reliable estimates are not available for this sort of leakage either.

Sources of Demand for Unauthorised Foreign Exchange: The demand for foreign exchange comes from various sources, such as trade, travel, capital transfers, study abroad, medical treatment, interest and dividends and royalty payments. Similarly, the government also incurs expenditure in foreign exchange on various counts. Under full and comprehensive foreign exchange control in India, foreign exchange is allocated centrally among competing claimants through a complex, tortuous and dilatory process. Normally, the entire demand for foreign exchange is not met through official allotment. Some residual demand, large or small, and some illegal heads of demand (such as, for smuggling) are always left out, which are met through the black market in foreign exchange.

The various sources of demand of unauthorised foreign exchange are: under-invoicing of imports; over-invoicing of exports; smuggling into the country; unaccounted foreign travel expenses; unauthorised transfer of capital abroad; unabsorbed expenses of offices abroad; and adjustments of claims of buyers or agents abroad.

I have already discussed in the foregoing the under-invoicing of imports and the over-invoicing of exports and how they give rise to the demand for unauthorised foreign exchange. I shall examine smuggling in the next chapter. Other sources of demand are self-explanatory and need not detain us here. We should, however, take particular note of the illegal flight of Indian capital to other countries. This is discussed briefly below.

Capital Flight: Capital flight adds to the flow demand for unauthorised foreign exchange. Further, these outflows of capital year after year have been quite sizeable. Rishi and Boyce (1990) have estimated that over the 16-year period 1971–86, the total capital flight amounted to US $21.1 billion in 1986, and that the cumulative stock of capital flight with imputed interest earnings (using the US short-term treasury bill rate as a proxy for the default-risk-free rate of average earnings) amounted to $29.6 billion. (These were equivalent, respectively, to 52 per cent and 71 per cent of the external debt of $40.4 billion accumulated during the same period.) The authors also estimated that during the 1980s, the exodus of capital from India was more than $2 billion per annum. This means that over the four years up to the end of 1990, the cumulative sum of capital flight in 1986 US dollars amounted to about $30 billion (more than Rs 75,000 crore at the current exchange rate of more than Rs 25 per US dollar) and more than

$42 billion with interest adjustments. The estimates are not error-free. How much they suffer from underestimation due to, say, the presence of smuggling, kickbacks, commissions, over-payment of freight and insurance with undisclosed rebate, and the unauthorised remittance of funds is hard to say.

Capital flown abroad has been used variously—partly to set up businesses abroad, partly to hold real estate and financial assets abroad, including bank deposits, and partly to finance smuggling, among other things. Swiss bank deposits, held by Indians represent, at best, only a small fraction of the total capital flight from India—the proverbial tip of the iceberg.

Thus, India has suffered, and still continues to suffer, not only from brain drain, but also from capital drain (capital flight in hard foreign currency). Without these two kinds of drains, the rate of growth of the Indian economy would have been much higher.

Black Market in Foreign Exchange

A part of the total demand for unauthorised foreign exchange is met directly through internal sources, as some firms generate their own supply of such foreign exchange through any one or more of the various sources discussed earlier, and is held abroad for ready use. The rest of the demand for unauthorised foreign exchange is routed to the black market in foreign exchange, which also attracts the bulk of its supply for sale. Such markets are operating in major port cities as well as in up-country urban centres, such as Delhi in India, with Bombay as its nerve-centre. These markets also operate outside India, in places like Dubai, Hong Kong, Singapore, London and New York. In the centres in India, interested parties know, by word of mouth, who the dealers in black foreign exchange are. In Bombay, most of the offices of the dealers in black foreign exchange, including the agencies of large and medium-sized companies, are concentrated in a small market. Here, illegal transactions in black foreign exchange of the value of Rs 1,200 crore are estimated to have taken place in 1984–85 (Chawla, 1985).

Like other markets, the black market in foreign exchange also operates through the price mechanism. Here, the relevant price is the rupee price of a specific foreign currency, say, the US dollar or British pound sterling. The excess of this black market price over the official exchange rate gives the black market premium, say, per US dollar. (When this premium is expressed as a percentage of the official rupee price per dollar, it is called the premium rate).

The black market premium (or its rate) affects both the demand for black foreign exchange as well as its supply. Other things being the same, more black foreign exchange is demanded (and less of it supplied) at a lower premium rate and less black foreign exchange is demanded (and more of it supplied) at a higher premium rate. In other words, the demand curve for black foreign exchange is downward sloping and its supply curve is upward sloping with respect to the premium rate. The premium rate is, then, determined by a rough balance between the demand and supply of black foreign exchange—a rough balance because this market is not an open, auction-type market. Other factors that militate against a single market-clearing price are the absence of big dealers in black foreign exchange who may make a market on their own account, the imperfect flow of information within as well as among various far-flung segments of the worldwide market, and so on. Yet, the price is determined within a narrow range. The variations over time in this price are largely governed by the degree of excess demand at the prevailing price. That is, this price goes up or down according to whether there is a positive or negative excess demand at this price. Through this price mechanism all the supply of unauthorised foreign exchange getting generated per unit time or released from past accumulations gets allocated among competing demanders, including its hoarders.

The premium on the official Re–$ rate of exchange has varied a good deal over time. Data on the black-market rupee rates for the US dollar at the end of the month are published regularly in various issues of *Pick's Currency Yearbook*. From these data, annual averages of the black-market rates can easily be computed and, given the official rupee exchange rate (published by the RBI), the black-market premia can also be easily calculated. Nayak (1977, Table 9) has done this and has also computed the premium rate (in percentage terms) over the official exchange rate, for the period 1961–62 to 1973–74. The results are one broad and useful indicator of the extent of the overvaluation of the Indian rupee, the seriousness of the foreign exchange situation and the heavy pressure on the rupee because of the large-scale black marketing in foreign exchange. Roughly speaking, the black market premium rate was about 50.0 per cent over the three years 1961–64; it rose to as much as 67.5 per cent in 1964–65 and to a peak of 98.5 per cent in 1965–66. With so much pressure on the Indian rupee, it was finally devalued on 6 June 1966 by 36.5 per cent, and the par value of Rs 100 in terms of the US dollar was reduced from US $21.00 to US $13.33 (or the Re–$ exchange rate was raised from Rs 4.76 to Rs 7.50).

The devaluation of the rupee did reduce the premium rate on dollars for the next three years (1966–69) to an average of about 40.0 per cent. But the next three years (1969–72) reversed the trend somewhat, with an average premium rate existing of about 48.0 per cent. This was presumably due to the increased demand for black-market dollars arising from increased smuggling. There was a perceptible decline in the average premium rate to 32.3 per cent for the year 1972–73. Thereafter, this rate has been relatively low for most of the years. The relevant data for the years 1973 to 1987 are summarised in Table 3.1.

The following points about the data in Table 3.1 may be noted:

1. We have no firm basis to assess the reliablity of the data in Column 2. According to this column, in only 4 out of 15 years (namely, the years from 1981 to 1984) was the black market premium rate more than 20 per cent. In the other eleven years, it was less than 20 per cent—with three years (1975, 1977 and 1980) having a premium rate of less than even 10 per cent.
2. Over the period covered in Table 3.1, the official exchange rate (Column 3) was placed on a 'controlled floating' basis—first, by linking it to the pound sterling (which was, itself, allowed to float from 23 June 1972) and then, from 24 September, 1975, by linking it to a 'basket of currencies,' supposedly including the US dollar, the British pound, the Japanese yen, the West German mark, and so on.

The factors operating on the demand and supply of foreign exchange in the black market (and their further determinants) have been too numerous and their interaction too complex. Some have already been discussed briefly in earlier parts of this section; others will be discussed in the next chapter, in the section 'smuggling'.

Table 3.1
Black Market Rate, Official Exchange Rate and Premium Rate for the US Dollar as Against the Indian Rupee

Year	*Black Market Rate of US Dollar*	*Official Exchange Rate of US Dollar*	*Premium Rate*
(1)	*(2)*	*(3)*	*(4)*
1973	9.21	8.13	13.3
1974	9.31	8.08	15.2
1975	9.60	8.94	7.4
1976	10.06	8.89	13.2
1977	9.69	8.90	8.9
1978	9.51	8.34	14.0
1979	8.74	7.81	11.9
1980	8.44	7.97	5.9
1981	9.85	8.04	22.5
1982	11.68	9.43	23.9
1983	12.09	9.77	23.8
1984	13.95	10.88	28.2
1985	14.57	12.51	16.5
1986	14.01	12.45	12.5
1987	14.57	13.05	11.6

Source: The figures in Columns 2 and 3 for the years 1973 to 1975 have been taken from *Pick's Currency Yearbook*, 1976. The remaining figures have been compiled by Dr Khan Masood Ahmad, using the following sources: Column 2: *Far Eastern Economic Review* (monthly issues); Column 3: RBI, *Report on Currency and Finance* (annual issues).

Note: Figures for Columns 2 and 3 are in Indian rupees. Figures in Column 4 are percentages.

Hawala Transactions

Purchase and sale transactions in black foreign exchange with delivery arrangements to designated parties are usually called *hawala* transactions in market circles in India, and a large part of unauthorised foreign exchange transactions are presumably carried out through them. These are generally transactions by word of mouth, and the sums are paid on the basis of correct references (*hawala*). Presumably, because of the verbal character of the mode (or *modus operandi*) of these transactions, they have come to be called *hawala* transactions. Another special feature of these transactions is that the verbal commitments made are fully honoured. Full faith in the honesty of the dealer is the basis on which *hawala* transactions are conducted. Failure to meet one's true obligations and any attempt at cheating by the *hawala* dealer are most uncommon, otherwise this kind of illegal business would not have flourished and would have soon died down.

Hawala transactions always involve the remittance of funds through non-official channels. It is different from the money-changer's business in which one currency is exchanged on the spot for another at the prevailing unofficial rate. *Hawala* transactions involve either the purchase or sale of foreign currency against payment abroad to a designated party. First, take the case of the purchase of, say, dollars transaction. Suppose a party in the US wants to remit funds to another party in India. The former has two options: either to remit funds through official banking channels or through some unofficial channel. Under the former, dollars will be converted into rupees at the official rate of exchange; under the latter, the conversion will be done at a premium, and it is this premium which is the main attraction for the black market sale of dollars. The dealer who purchases dollars in the US (mostly from Indians working abroad and desirous of remitting rupee funds in India) does not pay ready cash, as he has none there. He does not issue any written receipt for the sums received nor an order for payment of rupees of equal value in India. All that he does is to extend a firm verbal commitment to the seller of dollars to make an equivalent rupee payment (at an agreed rate of exchange) to the designated party in India. And, as already said, this leg of the transaction is honoured fully. Only then is the transaction said to be completed.

In the sale transaction (say, for dollars), the reverse happens. Anyone who needs a certain amount of dollars may purchase them in India against rupees in the black market. For this, he makes a cash payment in rupees at the prevailing black market rate. The *hawala* dealer, who has sold the required amount of dollars (for delivery abroad) at a premium, then arranges to deliver the amount at the agreed address and time. Again, what the dealer in question has sold is his *hawala* or promise to deliver a certain definite amount of dollars at the designated address and time in the US. (For this, he generally sends a coded message to his correspondent in the US). The transaction is completed when this promise has been executed.

The fore-mentioned *hawala* transactions in rupees and foreign exchange are illegal in India because of the existence of foreign exchange control here. But they are not illegal in most other countries whose currencies are bought and sold through these transactions, so that even business in these countries can be solicited through newspaper advertisements, offering a higher than the official rupee price for, say, dollars sold. In these countries, these transactions are open market (white, not black) transactions. The operators in India, however, operate surreptitiously. This is also true of their agents operating in various cities in India.

Towards Trade Liberalisation

Since March 1985, several steps have been taken to liberalise import trade, especially for exporters. I shall study below the main features of the policy measures under two sub-heads—measures prior to July 1991, and measures since July 1991.

Measures Prior to July 1991: The key feature of the measures taken since March 1985 has been export-linked import liberalisations. This was attempted largely through expansion of the OGL list of imports via inclusion of new items in this list, and the transfer of items from the licensed list involving quantitative restrictions. Also, in the liberalisation of imports, priority was given to the import of capital goods, raw material and components, and especially those needed for exports. Besides, there was selective tariff reduction, perferential access to imports for exporters, and various export-promotion measures, such as increasingly liberal Cash Compensatory Schemes, Duty Drawbacks and advance (import) licenses. I have already indicated in the foregoing how some of these promotional measures have been misused by unscrupulous traders in making black private gains.

Measures since July 1991: In the face of a severe balance of-payment crisis, raging inflation and the urgent need for large enough loan assistance from the IMF and the World Bank, several drastic policy measures have been taken since June–July 1991. Beginning with the downward exchange rate adjustment of 18 per cent in the dollar value of the rupee (making the dollar costlier by about 25 per cent in terms of rupees), which was designed to provide a substantial stimulus to exports, several trade policy reforms were also introduced. The more important ones are summed up below.

First, under the July 1991 trade liberalisation, a large part of administered licensing of imports was replaced by import entitlements linked to export earnings, while the Cash Compensatory Scheme and some other schemes for export promotion were withdrawn. These import entitlements, renamed Exim scrips, were freely tradable and attracted a premium in the market. For most exports, a uniform rate of 30 per cent of Exim scrips was made applicable, though some exports were entitled to higher rates. The Exim scrips could be used to import any item in the limited permissible list, like all OGL items for actual users and non-OGL capital goods which were not in the restricted list.

Second, the advance licensing system for exports was simplified.

Third, export houses were permitted a larger range of imports.

Fourth, the scope of canalisation for both exports and imports was narrowed.

Fifth, actual user requirement for the import of capital goods, raw materials and components under OGL was removed in October/ November 1991.

Sixth, established exporters were permitted to maintain foreign currency accounts and to raise external credits to finance their trade transactions.

Seventh, further measures towards trade liberalisation were announced in the Central government budget for 1992–93. The most significant measure was the total replacement of the Exim scrips (introduced in July 1991) by a more liberal 'dual exchange rate' system, based on partial convertibility of the rupee. Under the new system, 40 per cent of all 'foreign exchange' (forex) earnings—both in the form of export earnings and remittances from abroad—get converted into rupees at the official rate; the balance 60 per cent can be sold at market rates. (Foreign exchange earners are also allowed to hold 15 per cent of their receipts of forex in the form of deposits with banks). On 9 April, 1992, the rupee rates for one US dollar quoted in Delhi were: RBI buying rate, Rs 25.40; buying market rate, Rs 30.45 and selling market rate, Rs 31.70. It is expected that this will encourage exports greatly, also greatly reduce *hawala* transactions and capital flight from India. Overall, this is likely to add $2–3 billion to the availability of dollars over the year 1992–93.

On the opposite side, imports will be discouraged by the increased cost of free-market dollars. This has been cushioned only partly by the reduction in customs duties. Since the latter are still quite high, the temptation to under-invoice imports and finance them through the *hawala* market is still quite strong. Much will depend on the growth of exports. If this growth is mild and slow, the government will soon run out of its borrowed forex reserves and will not be able to go ahead with its eventual plan of full convertibility of the rupee. Immediately, the rising rupee-cost of dollars will make imports costlier, stunt industrial recovery, and push up the domestic inflation rate. This is a disheartening prospect. (Measures in the budget regarding the import of gold to discourage gold smuggling into the country will be discussed in the next chapter in the section on smuggling).

It may also be noted that the new trade policy is supplemented by measures to attract direct foreign equity capital and technology as well as portfolio investment into the country, with a view to modernise and globalise the Indian economy.

Eighth, the *new Exim policy*, effective 1 April 1992, virtually frees imports from licensing controls, barring those of consumer goods. Goods outside the two small 'negative lists' (comprising banned, restricted and canalised items)—one for imports and the other for exports—specified in the policy, can now be freely traded. It is estimated that under the new exim policy, only 5 per cent of the import items of non-consumer goods will be under licensing restriction. Till end March 1992, 40 per cent of this category of imports required licensing. Similarly, on the export front, 80 per cent of the restrictions have been removed.

The new policy has also virtually eliminated import canalisation, except for certain bulk and essential items, namely, petroleum products, edible oils, fertilisers and cereals.

The new policy aims at a stable trade regime. To this end, it will remain valid for five years, corresponding to the Eighth plan (1992–97). Necessary changes will be made once every quarter, and not on a continuing basis as in the past

As to the anti-black-income effects of the new policy measures, the following may be said:

1. The substantial elimination of import licenses and other trade controls has certainly reduced the opportunities for political-bureaucratic corruption and black-income generation.

2. The generally high customs duties are still enough incentive for under-invoicing imports, and financing a part of the imports with the help of dollars bought in the *hawala* market.
3. The dual exchange rate (with only 60 per cent of forex receipts allowed for sale at the open market rate) is conducive to the under-reporting of export earnings and a diversion of a part of the inward remittances of dollars to the *hawala* market. The increased and liberalised export incentives have also enhanced the scope for malpractices and fraud by unscrupulous traders.
4. Irrespective of the state of gold smuggling, there is still a lot of smuggling of narcotic drugs, synthetic fabrics, diamonds and a wide variety of high-value electronic and other goods to worry about.
5. Foreign exchange leakages, *hawala* transactions and corruption in the customs department and elsewhere continue to plague the economy, though they might have suffered some setbacks.

4

Sources of Black Income: II

Smuggling

Smuggling refers to the illegal import or export of goods. Only when there is complete free trade in goods of all kinds (including narcotics, and arms and ammunition) is smuggling, by definition, completely eliminated. But, for reasons of state policy pertaining to proctection to the domestic industry agaisnt foreign competition, government revenues, balance-of-payments (foreign exchange position) and ban on trade in goods which are considered to be hazardous to the welfare of society, the government in India has been following a policy of intensive control of the country's foreign trade through the medium of customs duties, physical controls (import licenses) and foreign exhange regulations. All these controls and tariffs invariably create profitable opportunities for trade by smugglers in several goods, the expected average rate of profit from smuggling varying a good deal across commodities to be traded and over time.

India has been facing the problem of both smuggling in and out of goods. Of the two, the former is several times more serious than the latter. So I shall concentrate mainly on this problem. We may note in passing, however, that the chief items of smuggling out have been silver, snake skin, antiques (mostly sculptures stolen from temples) and finished diamonds, some of which are also sent through under-invoicing of exports.

The smuggling of silver is an interesting case which demonstrates well the impact of market forces via net profitability from smuggling. Traditionally, silver was smuggled out of the country to pay for gold smuggled into India. On its own, too, the smuggling of silver out of the country was privately profitable, as the international price of silver was sufficiently higher than the domestic price of silver in India. But all this changed from the beginning of 1985. Since then, the international price of silver (evaluated at the black-market rate in dollars) has been much lower than the domestic price of silver in India, so as to induce the smuggling of silver into the country and to leave a handsome net profit margin for the smuggler after all his costs of smuggling have been fully covered. (The aforesaid price differential has varied roughly between 35 per cent and 66 per cent of the New York price of silver—based on data compiled by Dr Khan Masood Ahmad)

In value terms, the articles smuggled into India which have received maximum attention have been gold, synthetic yarn and fabrics, and wrist-watches and, during the 1980s, electronic goods (such as VCRs and video and audio cassettes). Gold, of course, has been a traditional item of smuggling. But, in value terms, it has not always been on the top of the list of items smuggled into the country. In recent years, synthetic yarn and fabrics have earned this distinction. Two other important items of smuggling are diamonds and narcotic drugs.

Smuggling is now big business. Its annual total value, which was variously estimated at a few hundred crore rupees during the 1960s, had already crossed the Rs 1,000 crore mark in 1974 and was placed at about Rs 1,200 crore for that year. There was a relative lull over the next approximately six years. It is thought to have picked up steam in 1981 and gone full speed ahead thereafter. For example, on the basis of classified official reports, unofficial but authoritative sources and the value of contraband seized by the customs department, the following estimates of the annual value of smuggling were hazarded (Praful Bidwai, *The Times of India*, 11 May 1983):

1981: Rs 2,400 crore to Rs 3,000 crore
1982: Rs 4,000 crore to Rs 5,000 crore

Bidwai's guess for 1983 was that smuggling had probably already crossed the Rs 7,000 crore-a-year mark. Only a year before, Bidwai had published a four-part investigative report, 'Smuggling on the West Coast,' in *The Times of India* (27,28,29 and 30 May, 1982). Based on this report and irked by the escape of a top smuggler (Bakhia) from a Goa jail, *The Times of India* (11 June, 1982), in its editorial entitled 'The Third Economy,' made the following pertinent observations:

1. that notorious smugglers have come to wield considerable power in the country; that they have succeeded in emasculating central monitoring, preventive and enforcement agencies, corrupting the administration in several states and turning the customs apparatus into a farce; that they have been able to do this with virtual impunity and, in many cases, with protection from powerful politicians and bureaucrats. Thereby they have inflicted incalculable damage on the integrity of the administration and the political system itself;
2. that contraband trade has become so large as to deserve the title of 'the third economy'. It runs into several thousand crore rupees. 'This could well be equal to the entire value of India's official exports or over 5 per cent of its national income';
3. that the 'third economy' has expanded at a high exponential rate and threatens to grow even faster unless drastic measures are taken to curb it. Its growth implies not merely a massive loss in revenue, running into hundreds of crores, in the form of import and excise duties as well as income tax and other imports. It also, and more ominously, involves the diversion of an appreciable chunk of gross domestic savings into unproductive channels. Additionally, it also involves the diversion and maluse of large amounts of valuable foreign exchange.

The 'third economy' (smuggling) has since grown at an alarming rate, with high-value drug trafficking and the smuggling in and out of diamonds becoming more and more important and the smuggling of gold also regaining high profitability, as discussed later. As a result, total smuggling may be currently (1989–90) running at the rate of at least Rs 15,000–20,000 crore a year, with a high growth rate of its own.

Earlier (almost up to the end of 1960s), smuggling was in the hands of relatively small outfits. Smugglers also used to operate on a relatively small scale. But, over time, as the opportunities for smuggling and the profitablility from it improved greatly due to several factors, such as the entry of new products (for example, synthetic fabrics and yarn, electronic goods—coloured TVs, VCRs and video and audio cassettes—and lately, narcotic drugs), high import tariffs and excise duties, and the development of highly favourable price differentials between domestic market prices and foreign prices of the potential items of smuggling, larger gangs or syndicates of smugglers have come to be organised. Almost all of them are based in Dubai. Some of them have come up from small beginnings and the reinvestment of past profits. Others have started with larger capitalisation. They are able to raise capital from outside sources as well, including banks in Dubai. Illegal, but fully reliable, insurance has also come to be organised, which sells insurance (against the risk of seizure or other losses) at the high rate of about 15 per cent of the value of the contraband. Then, at the Indian end, the clearing agents at the site of landing arrange for the clandestine delivery as well as warehousing of the smuggled goods at their own responsibility and risk. There are also 'disposal agents' in Bombay who work for big smuggling syndicates and look after the quick disposal (or distribution) of smuggled goods.

Contraband enters the country from practically all sides, and even by air. The most important entry points are, of course, located on the west coast, such as Daman, Kutch (in Gujarat), and of late, Goa, where big smuggling syndicates are strongly entrenched along with small smugglers, landing agents and their supporting staff of informers, watch and ward, transporters, drivers, and so on. Several other local people, such as those working at the local tea shops, and casual porters also depend for their extra earnings on the landings of contraband and the sudden spurt in activity at the place. Some look forward to a trip to Dubai (or some other place in the Gulf) in search of employment and high earnings. Most of the contraband is generally moved by road to Bombay, which has served as the main distribution centre in the country, and has the necessary infrastructure of a vast chain of traders, wholesalers, retailers and financiers, with countrywide links for the distribution of goods and the spread of information. Locally, smuggled goods are easily available in most regular and pavement markets and are sold at what appears as 'bargain prices'. Further, the relative geographical advantage of the west coast to the re-exporters concentrated largely in Dubai, with extremely liberal laws and well-developed specialised facilities for packaging and shipping the contraband to India (and Pakistan), also favours the Bombay area as the target destination for all manner of smuggling activity, despite heavy patrolling of the sea coast around Bombay by the Indian customs. These locational and organisational advantages are so highly valued that not only the goods from the West (especially gold), but also from Japan (such as synthetics and blended fabrics, electronic goods and watches) are routed in bulk through Dubai. Another large part of Japanese products comes through Hong Kong, Singapore and Bangkok.

In-and-out smuggling has also been conducted on India's border with Nepal, Bangladesh, Burma and Pakistan. Through Western tourists visiting Nepal, gold, electronic items, synthetics and several other goods are procured and smuggled into India. Goods in short supply and costlier in Nepal than in India are smuggled out to that country. Laxity in checks at the Indo-Nepal border helps this two-way flow of goods. This is broadly true of smuggling with respect to Bangladesh and Burma.

Till the early 1980s, smuggling on the Indo-Pak border was not of any special significance. But a sea-change has occurred since then, because of the growth in narcotics smuggling.

Several factors influence the volume and composition of smuggling, some operating mainly on the demand side, others on the supply side. The demand for smuggled goods—such as gold, synthetic fabrics, electronic goods (mainly watches, VCRs and TVs) and diamonds—comes mainly from the affluent sections of society whose income and wealth have grown rapidly over the last three decades or so primarily due to increasingly rampant black-income activities. This section of Indian society provides a large and growing market for smuggled foreign goods, with a craze for everything 'foreign'. High domestic costs, including high indirect taxes on inputs as well as finished products combined with relatively poorer quality Indian products, improves greatly the demand for smuggled goods. From this perspective, all the factors responsible for the growth of black-income activities in the economy also encourage the increased smuggling of goods in India *via* the demand factor.

The supply of smuggled goods and their composition is governed largely by the net profitability (net expected rate of return) from smuggling. The gross profitability from smuggling (of, say, gold) is given by the difference between the domestic price of gold and the international price of gold. But smuggling is not a costless operation. To arrive at the net profitability from smuggling, we have to take various costs of smuggling into account, namely, the freight cost, labour cost, interest cost of funds invested in the operation, the additional cost of converting rupees (the sale proceeds) into dollars (the currency of foreign operations) at the black-market rate, the risk-cost of seizure of the contraband by the authorities, covered by, say, the high insurance premium of 12 per cent to 15 per cent of the total value of the contraband said to be charged by the syndicates of private insurers, and so on. Thus, entering into the business of actual smuggling requires large capital, risk-taking and organising abilities, connections with the underworld and the authorities or men of influence in India, and full readiness to undertake all sorts of criminal activities.

Some of the factors governing the net profitability from smuggling are highly volatile. In the case of gold (and also of silver), this has been especially true of the two basic prices—the domestic and the international price of gold—and of the Re–$ black market foreign exchange rate. Correspondingly, the flows of smuggling have also adjusted themselves to net variations in them. Improved government patrolling and vigilance against smuggling has also, at times, brought temporary lulls in smuggling. But, most of the time, smugglers have tried to stay two steps ahead of the authorities by using faster speed-boats fitted with more and more sophisticated gadgets, very powerful walkie-talkies, telescopes and highly sensitive radars.

Smugglers may also change their routes, destinations, landing places for unloading their contraband cargo, their staff (including couriers), and also switch goods to be smuggled, depending on changed market conditions, their market intelligence and their own assessment of the net profitability from the whole operation.

From time to time, the government has adopted special measures to curb smuggling and leakages of foreign exchange from India. One special measure was adopted in December 1974 in the form of a new law, called COFEPOSA (Conservation of Foreign Exchange and Prevention of Smuggling Activities) Act. Under it, wide powers of arrest of suspected culprits were given to the concerned authorities. (Economic offenders could also be hauled up under MISA [Maintenance of Internal Security Act], 1974.) As a result, over time, alleged smugglers were arrested in large numbers under the new Act. But this did little to stem the growing tide of smuggling, especially after the middle of 1981. On the arrest of 124 alleged smugglers under COFEPOSA in a pre-dawn swoop in four states, the editorial comment in *The Times of India* (New Delhi, 4 July, 1984) on the subject is very telling.

The main points of the comments are summarised below: One, there is abundant evidence that smuggling is rising at an alarming rate and that a substantial amount of the remittances that used to come to India from Indians working abroad are now being diverted into the trade in contraband.

Two, there is vast evidence to show that the enforcement apparatus has been so completely bought over by the smugglers that the only effect of a hike in import duties now is to increase the amount of clandestine imports. (Thus, according to watch manufacturers, as the total of customs, excise and state sales levies on watches increased from around 70 per cent in 1978 to 174 per cent in 1983–84, the number of watches smuggled into the country has surpassed all previous peaks and is in the neighbourhood of six to seven million a year. This is broadly true in respect of the very heavy smuggling of synthetic and blended textiles.)

Three, the data on average value per seizure (ranging from Rs 9,000 in 1982 to Rs 16,000 in 1984) amply show that all that the customs have been catching are poor migrant labourers and sundry passengers trying to smuggle a camera or a VCR into the country. The big fish are totally absent from their net.

Four, the experience of the whole decade (1975–84) shows that the use of COFEPOSA has been infructuous in checking smuggling, as the government has not been able to prove even a single case against the scores who were arrested ten years ago. Besides financing politicians, smugglers buy up every bureaucrat and policeman that matters to them.

Five, the more effective course to fight smuggling is to drastically reduce its profitability, and to that end to reduce customs and local excise duty, and make Indian industry produce on a scale and at prices that enable them to survive with at most a 40 to 50 per cent protection.

But the chief accent of government policy continues to be on law-enforcement measures. Since 1985, it has tried to strengthen them further. Among other things, this includes improved patrolling of India's west coast and the better organisation of intelligence gathering, vigilance and the seizure of contraband. Besides, in March 1985, the government introduced a new scheme for customs and excise officials. Under this scheme, customs officials and their informers are given a reward of 20 per cent of the value of goods seized, and 10 per cent of the value of seizure is doled out on the spot by collectors of customs. (Earlier, the reward rate was only 3 per cent to 5 per cent and that, too, after a long delay.) But, for reasons already discussed in the foregoing, all these measures put together have not achieved much success against smugglers and smuggling. Besides, under the present judicial system, alleged offenders under the COFEPOSA for smuggling or illegal foreign exchange transactions running into several million dollars are able to procure anticipatory bail from courts, jump bail and make good their escape.

Smuggling has several harmful effects. Only a brief discussion of these effects is offered here. First and foremost is the large illegal outflow of foreign exchange induced as well as necessitated by the smuggling in of goods, as this has to be paid for in hard foreign currency. For a developing country like India, foreign exchange has mostly been in short supply and is one of the most scarce resources limiting its rate of economic development. Smuggling severely jeopardises its efforts at the planned use of its foreign exchange earnings, greatly encourages the consumption of luxuries (such as a large variety of electronic goods) by the rich, and their accumulation of precious metals and gold jewellery as forms of holding their black wealth. These assets are totally unproductive socially. Second, smuggling causes much loss of revenue to the government—through the evasion of customs duty, excise duty, income and wealth taxes. Third, the smuggling of manufactured goods (such as synthetic fabrics, electronic watches and other electronic goods) affects the expansion of production of such goods in the country, thereby adversely affecting the growth of industry and employment in the country. Fourth, the nexus of smugglers with the underworld and criminals, on the one hand, and some politicians and bureaucrats, on the other, degenerates government's decision-making and other activities and lowers political and social norms. Fifth, the large amount of funds amassed by smugglers are not put to socially productive use or investment, but are frittered away in luxurious consumption or reinvested to further expand their network of illegal activities. Here, special mention may be made of the illicit trade in narcotics which is already causing havoc to an increasing number of drug addicts in India and foreign countries. Sixth, like other black-income activities, smuggling further accentuates the prevailing disparities in the distribution of income and wealth.

A brief account of the smuggling of four selected commodities (namely, gold, synthetic textiles, diamonds and narcotic drugs) is given below.

Gold: Traditionally, India has been known to be a bottomless pit for precious metals—gold and silver. In a statement in the Rajya Sabha on 16 August, 1990, the then Union Finance Minister, Prof. Madhu Dandavate, had placed private gold hoards in India between 10,000 to 15,000 tons. At the then prevailing price of gold in India of about Rs 3,400 per 10 grams of standard gold (or Rs 34 crore per ton of standard gold), in value terms, the gold hoards amounted to the staggering sum of between Rs 340,000 crore and Rs 510,000 crore. Since India has been only a tiny producer of gold (with a current annual output of about 2 tons), its large demand for gold in recent decades has been met through smuggling. This domestic demand has been further boosted by the growth of black income and wealth in the economy, and the use of gold jewellery as a valuable asset for holding black savings and wealth. Besides, gold is also used as a hedge against inflation. This is over and above the traditional love for the yellow metal among Indian women. Besides, gold smuggling has been boosted by the growing nexus between the smuggling of drugs and gold since 1982 as the foreign exchange earned through trade in narcotics is used to finance the smuggling of gold into India.

The amount of gold smuggled into the country has varied over time from year to year. It has been affected greatly by the differential between the domestic price of gold in India and the international price of gold in rupees at the Re–$ black market exchange rate. Thus, after the US went off the gold standard in August 1971 and the official US support to the open-market price of gold at $35 per ounce was totally snapped, the price of gold in the world markets rose continuously and rapidly till it reached the peak of US $565 per ounce in September 1980 in the London gold market. The rise in the price of gold in India did not keep pace with this rise in the international price of gold. Consequently, the aforesaid favourable price differential for gold smuggling got continuously eroded, and even became negative for some time in 1980–81. This meant that the net profitability from the smuggling of gold into India was reduced, and substantially so during some years. So there was a comparative lull in gold smuggling for almost a decade (1972–81). The place of gold in the smuggling kit was taken up by other items (such as synthetic textiles, watches, transistor radios and other electronic goods)—all of Japanese origin and smuggled mostly from Dubai.

Gold smuggling started with a spurt again from the middle of 1981, with the large fall in the international price of gold (from a high of $565 per ounce in September 1980 to a low of $322 per ounce in March 1982), and the gradual rise in the domestic price of gold. These twin developments restored the net profitability of gold smuggling, which has persisted at a high level (with a gross profit margin of 40 to 60 per cent) practically all through the post mid-1981 period. Consequently, gold smuggling has also been characterised by a rapid increase, as indicated by most trade estimates. Gold smuggling was officially estimated at 100 to 250 tons for 1989–90. At the going average market price of gold of Rs 3,400 per 10 grams, this would have amounted to a value of Rs 3,400 crore to Rs 8,500 crore.

In order to curb gold smuggling, as a part of the budget proposals for 1992–93, from March 1992 the government allowed returning Indians and non-resident Indians to import a maximum of 5 kgs of gold per passenger, with an import duty of Rs 450 (revised down to Rs 220 only two months later) per 10 grams of gold, payable in foreign exchange earned abroad. It was argued that this legalised import of gold, if large in total amount in relation to the demand for it, would have several beneficial effects. It would, for instance, lower the domestic market price of gold, which would squeeze profit margins from the smuggling of gold, given the stable international price of gold, and discourage gold smuggling as well as the diversion of foreign exchange earned into illegal *hawala* transactions used to finance gold-smuggling operations. It was also hoped that the customs revenue (in foreign exchange) of the Central government would grow from the customs duty on gold imports, and that the lower domestic price of gold would help promote the export of gold jewellery and export earnings.

The immediate effect of the new gold import policy was, no

doubt, to lower the domestic market price of gold in only a few market sessions. But the effect was extremely transient. The market price of gold has been fluctuating only on a somewhat lower level. So its other wholesome effects summed up earlier have yet to materialise. On the supply side, the predicted legal inflow of gold in large quantities did not materialise. In several cases detected by the Indian customs, incoming passengers tried to smuggle in gold hidden in their luggage in various ingenious ways, and thereby escape paying the customs duty, while declaring only a small part of the gold with them and paying the duty. Some of them may have been acting as couriers for regular smugglers. It was also argued that 15 per cent customs duty (already cut to half from May 1992) was presumably too high, that so many NRIs and Indian returnees would not have foreign exchange of the equivalent of Rs 15 lakh for 5 kgs of gold. Further, they may not find easy buyers for this gold with after-tax money in India, and the profits from the gold import route cannot be repatriated. Consequently, the sale of surplus foreign exchange in the *hawala* market still constitutes an attractive alternative. Things are likely to change with the lowering of the duty.

On the demand side, gold continues to be in steady demand for jewellery, hoarding and as a hedge against inflation, especially from the holders of black wealth and their women. With growing black wealth and inflation, the price of gold in India is likely to show an upward trend. Therefore, the smuggling of gold may also continue, though at a somewhat lower level.

Synthetic Textiles: Since the end of 1974, synthetic textiles have come to be smuggled into India in an increasingly big way—so much so that in several years they constituted the single most important smuggled item in total value terms, higher than even smuggled gold. For example, Bidwai (*The Times of India*, 11 May, 1983) had estimated that the quantity of synthetic and blended fabrics smuggled into India during the year 1982 was as much as about Rs 3,000 crore.

Diamonds: Illegal trade in diamonds, in regard to both import and export, is very large in value terms and has been growing at a high rate, with a rapid growth in their legitimate exports. The latter were of the value of Rs 912 crore in 1982–83 and of Rs 4,400 crore in 1988–89. The proportion of illegal trade in diamonds to their legal exports has been variously estimated at one-third to one.

In diamond trade, besides smuggling, there is also much faking of invoices at the stage of both import and export. Smuggling into the country is very difficult to check, given the small volume and high value involved, unless it is supported by a first-rate intelligence network in London, Antwerp (Belgium), New York, Bombay, Surat and Navsari. Smuggling out and the under-invoicing of exports are also helped by non-resident companies which have been set up in Antwerp, New York and other trading centres abroad, which are tightly run by the controlling families. The transfer of funds abroad in foreign currency, rather than duty avoidance, is said to be the chief rationale behind the smuggling out of diamonds.

The diamond business offers vast opportunities for accounting jugglery. For example, a part of the imports can be diverted to the booming domestic market which, in 1982–83, was estimated to absorb diamonds worth Rs 200 crore. Wastage can be overstated to deflate profits and taxes on them. Rough diamonds can be grossly undervalued without much fear of detection. Undeclared diamonds can be smuggled out, and so on.

Narcotics: The drug menace reached India through smuggling from around the early 1980s. Initially, India was used primarily as a transit route from Pakistan to the West (Europe and the US) for drug trafficking. Later, the drug traffickers and couriers sought additional business in India as well, through induced drug consumption in the border areas of Punjab, Rajasthan and Kutch, and in Bombay and Delhi. Drug trafficking used to be carried out mostly from Pakistan where, in the tribal areas of the north-west, poppy is grown extensively and processed into heroin and smack (brown sugar). Some smuggling of drugs also takes place from the north-east part of India (from Burma and Thailand). Now India, too, has graduated into a leading producer of heroin, a large part of which gets sold in Europe and the US. In India, poppy is cultivated mainly in seven Uttar Pradesh districts (Barabanki, Ghazipur, Varanasi, Bareilly, Rampur, Shahjahanpur and Dehradun). It is processed into heroin in crude village laboratories in these districts, and sent to Calcutta for the international market.

In addition, a part of the cannabis legally cultivated in Madhya Pradesh and Orissa for medical use and research is processed into hashish.

The drug syndicates have established their network from Punjab to Bombay, and from production centres in Uttar Pradesh to Calcutta. The Pakistani drug syndicates arrange to supply the goods at agreed points on the Indo-Pakistan border, or even inside India. Once in India, the Indian syndicate takes over and arranges for the warehousing, packaging and transporting of the smuggled drugs through its own network of people. To avoid seizure, they continuously change their addresses (using fictitious names or aliases), *modus operandi* and packaging techniques. For the big racketeers of Bombay, Delhi and Calcutta, the truly hefty profits are made from their international operations—from delivering heroin or smack to their counterparts at the main drug centres in western Europe (such as Amsterdam, London and Frankfurt) and the US (such as New York). For this, the services of professional criminals with contacts in the airlines and customs, couriers from the exit points (Bombay, Calcutta or Delhi) to the destinations in Europe and the US, and intermediaries with local connections in these countries to do business and receive payment are suitably hired. At every stage of the operation risks are involved—the risk of getting caught red-handed. The big fish can escape by keeping their hands clean or by absconding. But, if the goods are seized by the authorities, it may mean a huge loss of potential profits, sometimes running into several crore rupees. Therefore, the big bosses engaged in multi-crore rackets involving large foreign exchange try to buy protection beforehand by bribing heavily the police and other law-enforcement agencies, and their political mentors. At times, they are even able to buy the active collusion of some politicians. In some other countries, such as Colombia in South America, the drug mafia has come to acquire such enormous wealth and power that it can hold the local government to ransom and change it at will.

In India's big cities, too, like Bombay and Delhi, the drug syndicates have their distribution networks, employing largely the lumpen part of the local population. Through their activities, new drug addicts get added to the drug market. To stem the rot of drug trafficking and drug taking in India, various drug activities (such as the production, manufacturing, sale, purchase, warehousing, transporting, concealment and consumption of narcotics) have been made punishable by law with years of rigorous imprisonment and heavy fines. But, the big sharks generally manage to escape, as they have been using drug money for financing politicians and developing lobbies in the bureaucracy, judiciary, police and other enforcement agencies.

Profits from drug smuggling and trafficking are earned both in foreign exchange and Indian currency. They are disposed of for further profits in a variety of ways. A part of foreign exchange is sold in the *hawala* market for rupees; another part is used to finance the smuggling of gold and other contraband items into India, thereby encouraging smuggling. The illicitly-earned Indian money is partly laundered into white money and invested in real estate, hotels and restaurants, private taxis, studios producing television serials, advanced as loans for film production, and so on. Some of the laundered money is invested in shell corporations that take over legitimate business corporations.

A strong nexus has also developed between narcotic smuggling and terrorism (now called narco-terrorism). Because of the relatively small bulk and very high value of the item, especially in the West, terrorists are drawn to drug smuggling to raise large sums of money to buy arms with and finance their other activities, whether it is terrorists in Punjab, Assam, or Sri Lanka.

Price and Distribution Controls

Price and distribution (P and D) controls have been an important feature of the economic scene in India since the Second World War. However, their importance in several sectors of the economy has diminished a good deal over the past fifteen years, especially since March 1982 when 'full' control over cement was replaced by 'partial' control or by 'dual pricing'. Whatever the contribution of such controls in keeping the price of essential commodities 'under control,' they have surely been instrumental in the making of large individual fortunes, both of the already rich and the new rich in business, politics and government. This has encouraged the beneficiaries to continue their forays in other areas of black operations, which have flourished with great rapidity. Indeed, the experience of operating in black markets and of the quick 'rents' earned therein have propagated a 'black market' culture, whose after-effects are neither short-lived nor die with the relaxation of P and

D controls, but manifest themseleves elsewhere, as exemplified by the extensive black markets in duty-evaded and smuggled goods. This comprehensive and long-lasting term effect of P and D controls, and the associated black markets, has not been fully woven into traditional economic analysis, although the phenomenon of black markets is well-recognised in it. I shall discuss very briefly these controls and their effects on black-operations in this section. (For a more detailed discussion, see Dagli Committee, 1979, Malyarov, 1983, Ch. 3, Kulkarni, 1984 and Government of India, Ministry of Finance, 1986.)

Price and distribution controls date back to the Second World War, when these controls were imposed on such essential commodities as steel, cement, foodgrains, cloth and sugar, to ensure their supply at controlled prices to the government for defence purposes. These war-time controls continued even after the war and Independence (1947) due to the unrelieved acute shortages of several essential commodities, such as foodgrains. These controls continued as a matter of planning strategy, necessitated by the emphasis on the development of heavy and basic industries and infrastructure under the five-year plans, especially since the beginning of the Second Five Year Plan (1956–61). It was thought that the supply of essential commodities would not increase *pari passu* with the growth in demand for them, occasioned by a step-up in the rate of investment and a consequent increase in income. P and D controls continued till about the mid-1970s due to Mrs Gandhi's reliance on the political support of the Communist Party of India (CPI), especially after the Congress party split in 1969. The Essential Commodities Act, 1955, which gave the government wide powers to impose controls on production, distribution, pricing and other aspects was already on the anvil.

The control regime underwent many changes. It was interspersed with brief periods of decontrol of some commodities, followed by the resumption of control in most cases, when their prices rose 'too much and too fast' and their supply position did not become comfortable. Over time, the scope and form of control also varied. For example, a system of 'voluntary price regulation' was introduced in the 1960s for some commodities, such as textiles and vanaspati. 'Dual pricing' (or partial decontrol) was first introduced in October 1967 in the case of sugar, under which the industry was required to sell 60 per cent of its output to the government at controlled prices (for distribution to the public), and the sugar factories were given the freedom to sell the remaining 40 per cent of their output in the open market. The system of dual pricing has continued ever since in the case of sugar, with a brief unsuccessful experiment of total decontrol during 1978–79 when, due to a sharp rise in the price of sugar, the producers of sugar (and *gur* and *khandsari*) are reported to have made huge profits and shared some of them with the party in power (the Janata party). The dual pricing system was later extended to steel in October 1973, and to cement in March 1982. A particular variant of dual pricing had long been in operation in the case of foodgrains (wheat and rice) and important agricultural raw materials (cotton and jute). Here, the government agencies bought these commodities in the open market and also allowed private traders to buy them.

Since the mid-1970s, there has been a marked and steady trend towards relaxation of controls. Several factors have led to this change in policy. Some important factors are the large accumulation of a buffer-stock of foodgrains due to the success of the Green Revolution; temporary improvement in the foreign exchange position, largely due to inward remittances of foreign exchange from Indians working abroad; improvement in the supply position of essential industrial products, arising mainly from increases in their domestic production; and a gradual change in the political ideology of the government towards liberalism. The public, however, experienced the real relaxation when P and D controls on cement were lifted and cement became freely available in the market, even if at double the previous control price.

Because of the aforesaid extreme diversity in price controls, no documentation or up-to-date compendium of the thousands of control measures and administrative rules has ever existed. During the height of P and D controls, this feature endowed the control administration with immense discretionary powers, which could be and were used by the control administrators to line their pockets and bestow special favours on bribers.

At present, while the price of most industrial goods is determined by the market forces of demand and supply, the price of a number of commodities is administered by the government. This is true *ipso facto* of all commodities produced by the public sector (for instance, coal, electricity, and rail, air and road transport), and of some essential commodities produced largely by the private sector (for instance, bulk drugs and formulations, and aluminium). The important change that has come about in price management is that rigid price controls have given place to price regulation. Under price regulation, administered prices are fixed and revised from time to time in a more flexible and consistent manner, taking into account increases in costs that might have occurred since prices were last fixed or revised, the level and cost structure of new plants with higher capital cost but improved technology and allowance for fair return on the net worth of enterprises. Thus, administered prices are designed to impart a degree of 'regulated flexibility' (which the intially rigid P controls had sorely lacked), as well as some short-period stability to these prices, and thereby to the price level as a whole as far as possible.

In factor markets, wages and salaries in the government, public sector enterprises, educational institutions and hospitals are administered prices. So are the interest rates of banks—the structure of deposit rates as well as of lending rates—and of other financial institutions. Rents of old urban properties, both residential and commercial, have remained frozen for old tenants under the Rent Control Acts passed by several state governments. This is one kind of price control which has not been relaxed, despite its obvious inequity. It confers special privileges and economic benefits in favour of one group of people (old tenants of such properties) at very low rents, even if they are millionaires, at the cost of another group of people (landlords, in the present case, whatever their economic condition) and discourages the construction of urban properties for the purpose of renting them out.

The process of fixing administered prices or revising them for cost neutralisation or other reasons has, in general, been tardy (with a few exceptions) and has allowed the government (and therefore the senior bureaucracy) much discretion and so much scope for lobbying. In the case of agricultural prices, from year to year the government fixes and revises the procurement price for wheat, rice and coarse grains, the minimum support price for pulses, oilseeds and cotton and the statutory minimum price for sugarcane and jute, on the basis of recommendations of the Agricultural Costs and Prices Commission. On the basis of the procurement price of foodgrains and the estimated handling and distribution cost of the government (which comes to somewhat more than 30 per cent of the procurement cost), the government announces the issue price of foodgrains (usually much lower than the average cost incurred) to the public and absorbs the loss as food subsidy (this was Rs 2,200 crore in 1987–88).

Effects of P and D Controls on Black Operations

Short-term P and D controls to meet unforeseen contingencies (such as war, drought and international price hikes, like that of oil due to cartelisation) have often been considered a necessary evil. The argument generally rests on the politico-economic judgement that their social benefits far outweigh their social costs. There is no well-tested hard empirical evidence on this score. However, this broad empirical judgement is shared by many economists in India.

P and D controls as an instrument of long-term planning for economic development are a different matter. Here, the micro-price policy in an overall macro climate of price stability has to be attuned to the interests of not only the consumers of commodities in short supply, but also to the interests of the producers. The shortages will tend to become endemic, unless producers are allowed remunerative prices, supported by measures to step up the rate of investment in them adequately, so that the gap between demand and supply is progressively closed. In the case of essential commodities (such as foodgrains and sugar), the public distribution system also helps to control the situation better.

All these are well-known and well-accepted positive features of the control system. But, in practice, P and D controls suffer from several harmful economic and social effects. I shall discuss them below.

Black Marketing: Black marketing is the most well-known and well-accepted effect of P and D controls. Narrowly defined, it means the sale of goods at higher than listed prices. Broadly defined, black marketing also includes all unaccounted sales, that is, sales without bills or cash memos. In trade language, these goods are called 'No.2 goods'. Goods sold against a regular bill or cash memo are called 'No.1 goods' or goods fully accounted for in the books of transactors. Over the years, the output and sale of No.2 goods (including smuggled goods and narcotic drugs) have proliferated greatly. They already represent a sizeable proportion of total output (supply), and are generally estimated to grow at a higher rate than the output of No. 1 goods. They also constitute the bulk of the wares of black marketing. The chief objective of the seller to supply goods as No. 2 goods is to avoid taxes—commodity taxes and income tax on profit from sales. Other No. 2 goods include non-declarable goods, such as smuggled goods, narcotics, and imitations of popular brands. Their supply infringes on the laws of the land.

Black marketing, narrowly defined, is basically an attempt to earn extra profit from the sale of a commodity at a price higher than the administered (or officially fixed) price. What makes the transaction black rather than white is the illegality involved in charging a price higher than the administered price. As traditional economic theory predicts, such black marketing emerges in a condition of shortage when the market is barred from clearing itself by raising the price, and an artificially lower price is fixed and kept lower than the market-clearing price even when revised or reset. Thus, black markets have emerged and flourised in India in all commodities under price control. Black-market premia have generally been an increasing function of the degree of relative shortage of a commodity under control, other things being the same. These premia have not remained fixed, but have fluctuated greatly over time and across commodities. Over the years, the commodities which have been much in the news for black marketing have been cement, steel, coal and paper. Other examples of commodities carrying black premia have varied from vehicles (cars, scooters and tempos) to cinema tickets, that is, virtually anything that has suffered from short supply even for a short period.

Black market premia have always been the product of market shortages, the overall climate of inflation and the reluctance of the government to allow adequate, periodic and timely upward revisions of administered prices, whether in the private or the public sector, even in the face of uncontestable evidence of the rise in costs adduced by government appointed tariff boards/commissions or the official Bureau of Industrial Costs and Prices (BICP).

Quotas and Political Patronage: Apart from the commodities covered by the public distribution system (such as wheat, rice and sugar), several other items have been distributed to the public through quota allotments. Prime examples are cement, coal and iron and steel, although several other commodities (such as molasses, ethyl alcohol, and various commodities imported by the State Trading Corporation for distribution among manufacturers, such as edible oils), have also been in great demand at administered prices. In most such cases, black markets developed in actual supplies as well as quota permits. Several unscrupulous persons, therefore, established dummy firms with only an office, a signboard and office stationery, but without any actual production, or production capacity, with the sole purpose of getting user quotas of commodities in short supply and making a profit from the sale of such quota permits in the black market, for which there has always existed a ready market.

The distribution of quotas and permits has always been an important instrument of the distribution of political patronage by important politicians in exchange for contributions to party and personal funds and political support. Where possible, government officials of influence also extract their own share of bribes.

Black Supplies and Leakages in Distribution: If a commodity is sold in the black market, there must be supplies to sell. Feeding the black market is done in several ways and through various sources, involving leakages in the government scheme of distribution. The trader can do it on his own only by manipulating his books of account, such as showing the sale at a controlled price to fictitious parties but actually selling the commodity in question in black. However, the black market is fed mainly by the manufacturers who under-report their output to the authorities (whether the commodity is fully or partially controlled, or not controlled at all). The key motive for under-reporting output is provided by the objective of tax evasion—evasion of excise duty and so of corporation tax, personal income tax, and so on. When black-market opportunities are open, this offers an additional incentive. The manufacturer works out an arrangement with his stockists/dealers, who pay a stipulated amount of 'on-money' (under-the-table payment) in advance to the manufacturer before the goods are despatched. Such on-money payments are pocketed by the senior management of a company, and do not swell the revenues and profits of the company. This is why administered prices leave companies short of investible funds, although their managements partake of the illegal profits from black marketing of their products.

Black markets are also fed by supplies pilfered from government stocks, stores and project sites. The pilfered supplies are made good by manipulating accounts, over-designing projects, or under-using the materials stipulated, and substituting superior materials with inferior materials (such as cement with sand, high-strength iron bars with low-strength iron bars and new gunny bags with used gunny bags). The instances and methods used can be multiplied. Special mention may be made here of the forced capturing of a part of output (as of coal at the Dhanbad coal-mines) by the use of strong-arm tactics by local toughs, under the protection of local politicians and the police.

Private sector companies are not totally free from thefts of goods and other leakages. But the extent of damage is thought to be relatively less due to greater vigilance and stricter action against wrongful acts of employees.

Smuggled imports of foreign goods have also been an important well-known source of black supplies.

Excessive Hoarding of Essential Commodities: Shortages of essential commodities get accentuated when trader-profiteers resort to hoarding them beyond authorised limits considered necessary for orderly and regular distribution. By cornering a large part of market supply through excessive hoarding, the hoarders are able to raise the black market price of these goods, sell the hoarded supplies at artificially high black prices, and make huge profits. To counteract such operations, the government has tried various measures, such as declaring the excessive holding of stocks of designated commodities unlawful, periodic raids on godowns, and intercepting the unpermitted physical movement of such goods. The banks have also been asked to exercise selective credit control against the stockholding of certain essential commodities. All these and other meaures, however, have had only limited success, and hoarders have mostly been able to make large profits from their operations without suffering much punishment in most cases, as they could almost always bribe their way out.

Political Corruption: I have already discussed the subject of political corruption in Chapter 2. I shall refer only to corruption generated by the control system under discussion. I have already drawn attention earlier to corruption in high places associated with the quotas of essential commodities, black-market sales by manufacturers of sugar, cement, paper, and so on, black-market sales of licences, quotas and permits, illegal hoarding of essential commodities in short supply, and of their inter-zonal movement in periods of restrictions on such movements. Many such activities have been carried on under one garb or the other, with the support and connivance of someone high-up in the government, administration or politics. Besides all this, there has been petty corruption on a large scale, in which government employees controlling the administration and local politicians have made much money in bribes—regular or occasional—from traders and small industrial producers.

The chief source of such petty corruption has been the way the control system was organised and the manner in which it operated for about four decades. This system is based on various acts, and rules under the acts, and several control orders, all of which provide necessary legal frame. The actual control system has been governed by thousands of notifications and amendments issued from time to time under the relevant control orders. They have covered various facets of production, distribution, stockholding and the pricing of any item under control, have been highly complex, long and couched in legal jargon, and have never been consolidated and brought up-to-date in any one comprehensive notification, even for a single commodity. The result was that even the senior officials responsible for administering controls were not fully aware of what they had to administer. Because of this problem, even a government committee (Dagli Committee, 1979) appointed to enquire into controls had to rest content with only a sample study of them.

If controls were hard to administer, the small traders and producers found them harder to comply with. The control system often required that they take out several licences, maintain regular books of account and stock registers, and display prominently in their shops the price and opening stocks of controlled commodities. The small trader found all this tedious, time-consuming and costly. In the absence of full and ready information and frequent changes in control conditions, they were liable to violate some rule of the control system. Some unscrupulous traders deliberately indulged in illegal practices to profit from conditions of shortage and bribed their way to safety. The system also allowed too much discretion to local officials. So they could and did use this discretion to harass businessmen under their charge in various ways, and extract bribes from them by open or veiled threats of fines or prosecution for violation of the law. Generally, businessmen, also found it cheaper and easier to pay bribes to the officials and local politicians for necessary protection than to try to understand and strictly fulfil all the complex requirements of the complicated control system. To a small businessman (or any ordinary person for that matter), the immediate official is the state or representative of the awesome power of the state.

To be effective, the control system should be simple, and easily administrable by the control authorities. It should be well-documented and up-to-date, and businessmen and the public should find it easy to comply with. It should also provide for its honest and efficient administration, and for the all-round surveillance of production, sale and price of controlled commodities. However, the system as it evolved over the years was haphazard and chaotic. It developed a multiplicity of controls and control organisations to meet the multiple objectives of policy, with some controls tending to neutralise others. The control administration, as it emerged, was neither honest nor efficient, nor trained in the complexities and ethics of control administration. The employees, recruited at least partly on political considerations, regarded their jobs as sinecures for milching business as best as they could. Over time, their numbers increased but not their work efficiency. The result was all-round corruption, inefficiency and a waste of resources, not only in control administration but also in the economy as a whole through official obstructions, long delays in the grant of sanctions, permissions and actual supplies of inputs.

Waste and Distortions: In most cases, administered or control prices tend to be fixed at levels lower than the market-clearing prices. (This follows from the logic of P and D controls, which are imposed in the first place to arrest the rise of market prices.) Further, due to the sticky nature of these prices, the price advantage to the buyers of these commodities and the price disadvantage to their producers widens progressively under any on-going inflation. This results in a large number of distortions and a waste of real resources.

First, the waste occurs when resources are not used according to their true social cost but according to the low concessional prices paid. Thus, much excessive or wasteful use of such goods as cement and iron takes place in government as well as private construction and big projects.

Second, in cases where the administered items are produced by the public sector and a large part of the output is consumed in the private sector (for instance, electricity), the underpricing of these items (especially for bulk consumers or the politically favoured) has meant unwarranted subsidisation of the private sector by the public sector. (On top of this, theft of electricity is quite common and large groups of agricultural consumers refuse at will to pay electricity charges, imposing a heavy cost on the already loss-making state electricity boards, such as of Uttar Pradesh.) In several cases, such subsidies have contributed to the losses of the PSEs. In the ultimate analysis, these losses are absorbed by 'excess' deficit financing by the government. (Excess means more than what the economy can absorb at stable prices when the economy is growing along its maximum feasible growth path; see Gupta, 1979, Chapter 2.)

Third, P and D controls promote shortages in industries covered by them by affecting profitability in these industries (except through black operations), and thereby both the capacity and the willingness of firms to invest for the modernisation of plant or for capacity expansion. This has occurred in the case of several industries in the past, such as cement, sugar and paper. The shortage of investible funds with most PSEs (partly due to the uneconomic administered prices of their products) is well-known and has been one of the main reasons for the non-fulfilment of the public sector investment targets of the country's five year plans.

One related adverse consequence of P and D controls has been distortions in the investment pattern. Private firms generally prefer to invest in industries with high expected profitability and which are relatively free from controls. As a result, the production capacity of controlled basic and essential commodities suffers, while that of the less- or non-essential commodities flourishes. This is further encouraged on the demand side by the high and growing inequalities in the distribution of income and wealth, itself a consequence of the pervasiveness and intensity of black operations. This has greatly distorted the commodity composition of industrial output and of imports (including smuggling) in the country.

Fifth, the distribution of gains from P and D controls has been highly uneven. The small users of controlled commodities (especially cement, iron and steel, and coal) without much political influence have often been forced to meet a varying part of their needs for such commodities at inflated black-market prices due to inadequate allotment of quota to them and that, too, after much time, effort and bribery, unreliable supply schedules, and supplies of indifferent quality. However, the big and the influential users have been able to procure more than the requisite quota of such commodities, and profit from their sale in the black market.

It needs to be understood that the gains from black marketing have not gone entirely to the trader merchant. They have been shared by the manufacturer, on the one hand, and the politicians and officials on the other—the latter through bribes for ignoring violations of law and providing other modes of protection against detection, and the conviction of crime in the court of law. The manufacturer's access to black-market gains is not well-publicised, as he operates behind the scenes. But, it is widely held that in some industries, such as cement and paper, the manufacturers have been collecting at least a part of the black-market premia (called 'on-money' in trade parlance) in advance from their dealers/stockists for supplies to them (see Dagli Committee, 1979). This has been possible because (*a*) the dealers/stockists have had long business relations with the manufacturers, and would like to develop them further, and (*b*) a manufacturer can hurt or oblige, and thereby discipline, a recalcitrant dealer by disturbing or even choking off its supplies to the latter. The dealer, therefore, falls in line and raises his black-market price accordingly to recover all his outside payments, with profit, from the customer.

Industrial Licensing

Another important source of black income and wealth in India has been industrial licensing. This has held the large-scale industrial sector in the country under its shackles for forty years (1951–91). No doubt, its rigors were somewhat relaxed during the 1980s, especially since early 1985. However, the relaxations made were of a cautious and *ad hoc* nature within the general framework of industrial licensing. These amounted to no more than merely tinkering with the 'industrial licensing system' (ILS), which was otherwise left untouched. Major changes were introduced with the New Industrial Policy of the government announced on 24 July 1991, under which the industrial licensing requirement was fully withdrawn for all large-scale industries, except for 18 industries placed in Annexure II for which licensing continues to be compulsory. These 18 industries related to security and strategic concerns, social factors, hazardous chemicals and overriding environmental factors, and items of elitist consumption. They include coal, petroleum, sugar, animal fat and oils, cigars and cigarettes, motor cars, paper and newsprint (except bagasse-based units), electronic aerospace and defence equipment, hazardous chemicals, drugs and pharmaceuticals, and consumer electronic items (like colour TVs and VCRs and washing machines).

In this section, I shall discuss how the ILS operated in the past, insofar as it was instumental in generating black income and wealth, and reponsible for their highly skewed distribution. These effects, after all, are not short-lived. They have drastically altered the initial conditions of all black operators in the field. Thus, their present and future will continue to bear the marks of their past (for a critical evaluation of the organisation and working of the ILS, see, among others, Hazari, 1966, 1967; Bhagwati and Desai, 1970; Dutt Committee, 1969; Goyal, 1979; and Corporate Studies Group, 1981).

The ILS has also affected Indian industry since 1951. Whereas the overall industrial and economic policy of the government has boosted India's industrial development, the ILS *per se* has been responsible for constraining the rate of this development, for strong distortions in the associated industrial pattern and for the differential growth of several old and new industrial houses and firms. The complicity of the government and the leaders of the ruling political party at the time in the matter should not be underplayed.

Industrial licensing was adopted in 1951 as a method of regulating large-scale industrial investment to make it conform to the priorities and targets of planned industrial development envisaged in the ongoing five year plan, and to ensure that scarce national resources were not committed to the production of less important goods. At the time, it was believed that the market forces, guided purely by the profit motive, could not be relied upon to yield a socially-desirable pattern of large industrial investment. Two subsidiary objectives of industrial policy (presumably not pursued vigorously under the ILS) were greater regional dispersal of industry, and the prevention of monopoly and the concentration of economic power.

The authority to regulate large industry was enshrined in a

comprehensive new act—the Industries (Development and Regulation) Act (or IDRA), 1951. The industries subject to the Central government regulation under the Act were listed in a schedule, amended from time to time. The regulation of these industries required (*a*) registration of the existing units, and (*b*) taking out of a license to establish a new undertaking, for 'substantial expansion' of capacity in the existing line of operation, or to start manufacturing a new article. Small-scale industries were not required to obtain a license. Besides registration and licensing, the IDRA also conferred several other powers on the Central government, such as intervention in management and control as well as the pricing and distribution of scheduled industries.

To administer the ILS, the Directorate General of Technical Development (DGTD) was established. The DGTD functioned as the real workhorse of the ILS, even monitoring the implementation of industrial licenses. It carried out the 'techno-economic' evaluation of large industrial investment proposals for licenses, and proposals for foreign collaboration and loans for approval. Besides, there was an inter-ministry Industrial Licensing Committee (ILC) which met at regular intervals to approve or reject applications already processed by the DGTD.

The practical functioning of the ILS has attracted much criticism. I shall not go into the details, as the focus of my discussion is limited to only the black-income effects of the ILS. These effects, however, are intertwined with other effects and can be viewed only in relation to the working of the whole ILS. The following brief discussion will illustrate the point.

The central criticism of the ILS has been twofold. First, that by putting up barriers to the entry of fresh capital and enterprise in large industry (through licensing requirement), it slowed down considerably the rate of investment in such industry. Second, that it favoured a few large industrial houses (LIH) with well-established political and bureaucratic links, to the relative disadvantage of other new and smaller firms without much political clout or bureaucratic influence, thereby promoting economic concentration in the economy. Both the effects were linked.

The first point to note is that the ILS had allowed much discretion to the bureaucracy in charge of it, and to the political executive in the government above it. This discretion arose primarily from the fact that the ILS did not follow any explicitly-stated objective criteria for the grant or rejection of licenses, or the conditions attached to them. In the absence of these criteria, the DGTD and the ILC were free to use *ad hoc* criteria and discretion in their work. This offered immense opportunities to politicians and officials to reap private benefits and contributions to party funds, in return for special favours, such as granting licenses expeditiously and without demur. Firms whose applications for licenses or other kinds of approval were not cleared and subjected to long delays and enquires had no other recourse but bribes to get the necessary clearance.

Another feature of the ILS, common to the functioning of all government offices in India, was excessive delay and red-tapism in the process of clearing applications for licenses. This was easily done by raising several queries and objections, and seeking clarifications and explanations about some of the individual pieces of information in an application. This was not done all at once, especially if the application was handled by more than one desk. In addition, even a simple letter and its despatch could take a few weeks. Further, certain clarifications had to be certified by a designated competent authority. Thus, for a capital goods import license, which was an essential adjunct of an industrial license, the applicant was required to procure an 'essentiality certificate' from the Director of Industries and an 'indigenous non-availability certificate' from another concerned organisation. These organisations took their own time to issue the required certificates, and their officials had to be generously placated to do their duty.

Under the bureaucratic system of work organisation and the associated division of labour and hierarchical structure of authority, more than one official is supposed to scrutinise various aspects of an application, without anyone overstepping his authority. Also, a fixed sequence is supposed to be followed, in which a file moves from one desk to the other and to higher officials in the hierarchy. In the resulting red-tape, every one in the office moves at his or her own pace, knowing fully well that, unless pushed by someone higher up, he can, at least, delay greatly the file from moving further by going slow or, worse, by raising any number of awkward objections or deliberately misplacing a file. Thus, the power of obstruction and delay enjoyed by officials in the system is immense and frustrating to the applicants. It is this power and its knowledge to all concerned that enables officials to extract bribes for themselves, their associates and bosses.

In such a system, each aspirant for a license also tries to 'beat the system' in the only way open to him—by bribing directly, or through professional middlemen, the officials concerned down the line, or some key official or a political heavyweight who has promised to see the case file through (and share with others, if needed, the bribe negotiated), or someone higher up in the government who could instruct the licensing authorities to do his work expeditiously. Big houses are known to employ full-time liaison officers. These officers keep the senior company management fully posted with the progress in their cases, seek guidance in regard to specific difficulties or objections, advise necessary action (such as timely intervention by a friendly minister), and likely future policy changes. Big houses also maintain company guest houses in New Delhi, Bombay, Culcutta, hill stations and a fleet of company cars to oblige the influential, and arrange occasional get-togethers in five-star hotels where selected officials and politicians are honoured guests (see Kochanek, 1974).

It was widely held that most of the delays and hurdles in the issue of licenses were deliberate, and that they were tactics or methods being used to extract bribes from the applicants for licenses and to keep the scarcity value of such licenses sufficiently high. If the issue of licenses was fully streamlined, simplified, criteria-based and reasonably expeditious, the discretion and importance of the licensing authority and the 'higher-ups' in the government and politics would have diminished or disappeared, and an important source of bribes and party funds would have run dry.

The second feature of the working of the ILS was that it offered considerable scope for favours to be granted, most of which went to large industrial houses (LIH) and, among them, to a few prominent ones, especially to the Birlas. The issue of large industrial houses getting undue advantage under the ILS was enquired into in detail by the Dutt Committee (1969). In the Committee's view, although there was sufficient justification for a disproportionate share going to LIH in a few cases (based on technical reasons, the large investment required and the willingness to invest), in a large number of cases, there was no such justification. For example, there were cases of the issue of multiple licenses to the same house (in the name of different firms belonging to the house) in a given industry; cases of licenses for substantial expansion to an LIH even before it had implemented the initial license; cases where large capacities were granted without techno-economic necessity, and to a dominant undertaking in an industry (razor blades) which strengthened its 'product monopoly'; and cases when licenses were granted to the same house for industries of various kinds, purely on the basis of its ability to find influential foreign collaborators.

In addition, LIH also got special favours through various routes. One, by procuring advance information, they could apply for licenses well in time to take advantage of 'the first-come first-served' approach normally followed by the licensing authority in the disposal of applications. Late-comers were denied licenses on the grounds that the capacity to be licensed in an industry had already been exhausted.

In a large number of cases, an understanding was reached in advance between the government and selected entrepreneurs for setting up plants in designated industries. The grant of a license, then, was a mere formality. This was true, for example, of the aluminium project of the Birlas at Rihand (Uttar Pradesh).

Two, in several cases, licenses were issued to LIH even when the items were on the 'banned list' of the government, or the substantial expansion of their production capacities without license was simply ignored and not penalised.

Three, favouritism was displayed brazenly when, under special instructions of higher authorities, the applications of particular applicants were disposed of with great speed in a matter of days and, in one exceptional case (Pure Drinks, New Delhi), in only one day. This was done by suspending normal procedures and enquiries precedent to the grant of a license. In some other favoured cases, the scrutiny of applications would be superficial and inadequate, and the applicants would also be granted enough foreign exchange for the import of capital goods.

Four, in several cases, on the strength of instructions from higher levels, earlier decisions of rejection were reversed. Some houses even got licenses withdrawn from other firms and given to them.

Five, some LIH forced the government to issue licenses merely on the strength of the 'letters of intent' issued to them earlier, and on the strength of offers of foreign collaboration and loans.

Six, in some cases, the politically influential got away with licenses purely on the basis of illusory claims of special advantages, such as low foreign-exchange requirement. In several cases where the licenses issued carried various obligations or conditions, these conditions mostly remained unfulfilled and the government could not enforce them, since it had neither a well-organised monitoring outfit nor the necessary legal authority to enforce the conditions.

Seven, several houses, especially that of the Birlas, developed the practice of submitting several applications for a license each for the same product through various firms controlled by the house, obtaining a number of licenses while implementing only a few. Thus they were able to keep other firms out of an industry on the ground that 'no scope' was left for them to enter under the extant five year plan. That is, they were able to pre-empt a large part of the licensed capacity in an industry for themselves. This acted as a barrier to the entry of new firms in that industry and restrict market competition.

Thus, the ways and means of gaining/granting licensing favours were many. Indeed, obliging powerful politicians and officials got the necessary recompense for themselves and the ruling political party from the beneficiary industrial house. Thus, a strong nexus had come to develop between 'big capital' and 'big government' through industrial licensing, which involved high-level political corruption and bribery.

The working of the ILS adversely affected industrial planning in India. Under it, or despite it, the pattern of industrial development in the private sector realised over time was not in accordance with the Plan targets and priorities. Thus, actual new capacities in large industry were very different from licensed capacities, which were different from planned or target capacites; and actual outputs had diverged greatly from approved capacities in both directions, up and down. Both the underutilisation of capacities and 'over-production' (in several cases, exceeding even twice the capacities licensed, and mostly in socially non-essential industries, such as alcoholic beverages) were quite common. In respect to capacity creation, there were cases of both shortfall in capacity creation and cases of installation of excess capacity over the licensed capacity.

The former arose from non-implementation of licenses for several years without revocation. The setting up of unauthorised capacity later got recognised by the government through the allocation of raw materials and power, on the basis of actual capacities. Excess-capacity creation was found to be very common in the case of less essential consumer goods with brighter profit prospects. Over time, all these practices resulted in much unplanned allocation of scarce investible resources. They also led to product monopolies and the increased concentration of economic power in the hands of LIH, who had indulged in the aforesaid malpractices on a large scale.

How did all this come about? I have already mentioned the considerable political clout of large capital (LIH), political-bureaucratic corruption and the shortcomings of the ILS procedure. Besides, the monitoring of the implementation of industrial licenses was highly deficient. The DGTD, besides having the responsibility of project evaluation and approving industrial licensing, was also burdened with the task of monitoring the implementation of industrial licenses. The government did not organise any separate machinery to monitor the actual implementation of licenses, to ensure that the actual capacities installed were in accordance with the terms and conditions of the licenses, and to see that the unused licenses were surrendered or revoked expeditiously. Such a monitoring system would have required an efficient, standardised and quick reporting system, prompt analysis of reports received, and quick remedial action against violations or evasions, with the full authority and backing of the government. However, such a comprehensive monitoring system did not exist. So violations mostly went undetected and, when detected, were either explained away by the licensees, and excused by the authorities, or were time-barred for penal action, if the detection was not within one year of the issue of the license. In fact, big companies with their political clout could successfully resist government directives on such contentious issues as the correct measure of licensed capacity, reserved items for the small-scale industry, export obligations attached to an industrial license, and so on. They did this by exploiting various loopholes and ambiguities in the ILS through continuous legal battles, or by using political influence. The end-result was substantial divergence between the actual and planned industrial pattern, and thus a serious failure of industrial planning and the

ILS. The resulting distorted industrial pattern reflected the overall dominance of the market forces over the imperfectly planned and executed state regulation of the large industrial sector.

Under the ILS, industrial licenses were keenly sought after by industrial houses, old and new, for the *benefits* which flowed from them. First and foremost, in the absence of free entry in large industry, the government's permission to establish a new undertaking, or for the substantial expansion of an existing one, or for the manufacture of a new article in the form of an appropriate license was a necessary precondition. Therefore, for an industrial house to grow fast and maintain an eminent position in industry and the economy, it had become essential to procure licenses in various industries. The establishment of new industries and new undertakings, when run efficiently, gave them high profits and much political clout. In the highly protected Indian market, with its large and growing economic size and reliance on government assistance, practically all industrial houses have made economic fortunes of varying sizes. The excess or surplus profits made by them on account of government-created artificial scarcities through industrial licensing have been called 'rent' in Economics. Such rent-earning opportunities greatly boosted the demand for licenses.

The rents earned by industrial licensees were further enhanced by the liberal government grant of priority quotas of goods in short supply (such as steel, cement, coal and various imported raw materials) for their industries and at officially-controlled prices. Generally, a licensee would overstate his demand for such goods, and the 'smart' ones would get them sanctioned in full. Since the official prices would be lower than the black-market prices of these goods, they would carry a premium. The extra quantities, when sold in the black market, fetched them handsome extra profits or rents. Since these rents remained undeclared and therefore tax-free, their market value got further enhanced. Moreover, a state government, in order to attract industry to its state, would offer large areas of land of his choice to the industrialist to set up his factory at cheap rates, besides assuring him of an adequate supply of electricity and other facilities. Import licenses for the import of capital goods, spare parts, intermediates, raw materials, the possibility of foreign collaboration and assured long-term and short-term institutional finance have been many other attractions and benefits. Import licenses and foreign exchange allotments have also been big premia-earners in the black market.

Other Sources

Urban Real Estate

Transactions in urban real estate generate a large amount of black income, guesstimated to be more than Rs 10,000 crore annually. The transactions include the sale of old and new properties, 'general power of attorney' sales which do not require registration in court and so escape the high stamp duty payable on registered sales, encroachments on public land, acquisition of raw land for resale as housing plots, developments of this land for setting up a colony and the sale of plots or houses or flats constructed on it, and exceeding the legally permissible limit of the built-up area on a given plot of land. Many kinds of frauds are perpetrated in this business. One common feature is understating the value of the transaction and thereby evading a large part of the tax liability. This feature converts the gains made in the transaction into black gains. In all real-estate deals, property brokers (with contacts in officialdom) play an important role.

Another common practice is the under-reporting of rents received. Besides, property owners charge new tenants large amounts of interest-free advance, a security deposit or a non-refundable lump sum (called *pugree* in Bombay) while renting out their properties. However, the black income made in this way is small and scattered so it shall not be discussed here. The bulk of large black gains in urban real estate are made in the outright sale of real estate. It is this aspect that I shall discuss briefly below.

In metropolitan cities like Bombay, Calcutta, Delhi, Madras and Bangalore, in particular, and all urban areas in general, the growing scarcity of urban land due to the mounting pressure of urbanisation, and the continuing general inflation in the country coupled with opportunities for the relatively safe placement of black income and wealth in urban real estate, have made their prices soar everywhere. This has caused much speculation and attracted big money, which has exacerbated this trend further.

The very high rise in the price of real estate in big cities has thus been both the cause as well as the effect of high speculation in real estate. The associated high rates of capital appreciation realised are uniformly under-reported, turning the realised capital gains into black gains. The big gainers are mostly the already rich.

To counter the tendency to understate property values in sale deeds in big cities, the government amended the Income Tax Act in 1972 and, under the new Act, the government could buy grossly undervalued high-value properties and auction them off at a profit. This did not have the desired effect till the Act was amended again in 1986, when it provided for the pre-emptive purchase by the government of the properties whose true high values are grossly understated in sale proposals. This has had a relatively more salutary effect, though still very small. Some land might have been purchased *benami* to avoid tax liability.

Several malpractices are also associated with the acquisition and development of raw land for urban use and its actual utilisation, generating large amounts of black income, appropriated by only a few land developers. For the expansion of big cities in general, and for other public uses, the government and its agencies are authorised by law in most states to acquire land in rural areas from its owners. For this, the concerned authority issues a notification and individually notifies each owner about the government's plan to acquire his land at a price determined by the authority. The rate of compensation as well as the time of acquisition are decided by the authority. The former may be a small fraction of the going market value of raw land in the area, and actual acquisition may not take place for several years after the date of the notification. In the meantime, land developers, specualtors and other knowledgeable high-ups get into action quickly, buy up whatever land is available at a relatively cheaper price, and then exert pressure and influence on the authorities to fix a remunerative price of land in the form of adequate compensation to farmers whose land is proposed to be compulsorily acquired. Once acquisition for a particular area is announced, the price of land around that area also goes up, and the speculative demand for land in the area suddenly shoots up. The first purchasers of land, then, may sell off the land they had bought earlier and make quick profits. Since these transactions are always registered at grossly understated prices, the cost of stamp duty paid for the registration of land deals and any income tax due on the under-declared capital gains is kept as low as considered safe. Moneyed persons with the right connections are said to have made large profits quickly (running into several crores of rupees) from such deals and shared them with their contacts among the officials and politicians.

Large profits are also made by influential builders in big cities in several other ways, for instance, by constructing unauthorised markets in busy commercial districts of a city, getting them approved later, grabbing public land with the connivance of powerful local politicians, and putting up hotels and guest houses, and so on. In the past, private unauthorised housing colonies have also been put up, and housing plots of undeveloped land sold to gullible middle-income families. The colonies, being unauthorised and set up on undeveloped land, lack common civic facilities. The residents face the threat of demolition of their structures by the local authority. They live in the hope that their colony will be regularised by the government on the eve of next general elections. Powerful local politicians have encouraged and nursed encroachments on public land through clusters of *jhuggies* and *jhopdies* (make-shift hutments) that serve as their vote banks in the elections.

The role of 'black money' in the acquisition of urban real estate is substantial, whether it is for the purchase of old properties and their renovation or the construction of new ones, or the building of 'farm houses' with luxurious rest house facilities and comforts by affluent local businessmen, retired bureaucrats and military officers. In posh localities where top business and other rich families reside, the stamp of their affluence gained largely from black operations of various kinds is clearly visible in the life-style of their residents.

In the construction of new properties, builders play a very important role. As powerful oligopolies, they control a sizeable part of new building construction in a city. They enjoy close contacts with politicians and bureaucrats through regular pay-offs and offers of prize allotments to the latter. They also serve as conduits for the safe utilisation of black funds.

In Bombay, huge capital gains in urban real estate are made in yet another way. For example, official land records here are tampered with to show the falsely increased area of a plot from what was originally recorded in the land survey. Given the Floor Space Index or FSI (peculiar to Bombay), which determines the maximum built-up area for a plot of land of a given size, the 'official' increase in the size of a plot enables the builder to construct a much larger carpet area and earn crores of rupees from the sale of the extra built-up area on the same plot of land. In a city like Bombay with a huge demand for property, hundreds of crores of rupees of black money floating around, and an acute scarcity of vacant land, forging extra area in this manner through fraud has been widely practised. In such deals, the kingpins and main beneficiaries have been Bombay's 'real estate mafia', which includes big builder-contractors, financiers (from black-money hoards, including smugglers), and property dealers. They buy up the connivance and services of government officials in the land records department and other places concerned with the approval of building activity in the city and, above all, of powerful politicians. This practice is proving to be socially very harmful. It has greatly nullified all efforts at town planning in Bombay. The result has been more congestion, greater traffic bottlenecks, a perversely skewed distribution of job locations, and a higher burden on the already overstretched urban infrastructure. The proposals to officially raise the FSI fall in the same category of socially harmful measures, and for the same reasons summed up in the foregoing.

Another method followed by the government of Maharashtra to meet the ever-burgeoning demand for urban housing in Bombay is to dereserve prime land earmarked for public use, such as schools, colleges, hospitals and public parks, and to make it available at cheap rates to private developers for residential and commercial construction. In the process, large sums of money running into hundreds of crores of rupees change hands between the developers and smuggler-financiers, on the one hand, and politicians and bureaucrats, on the other hand. This shows that a strong nexus exists between the two sides.

The developments summed up in the foregoing have accentuated the disparities in the distribution of wealth in general, and of urban housing in particular, to the disadvantage of wage and salary earners without enough black income and to the advantage of black operators. As a result, social inequity in the field of urban housing has become more and more acute over time.

Leakages from Public Expenditure and Property

Leakages from public expenditure and property are common all over India. The two main channels of such leakages will now be briefly discussed.

Pay-offs or Cuts: At various levels the government is a heavy purchaser of machinery, other equipment and stores of all kinds for civil as well as defence purposes. Besides, the government spends heavily on the construction of irrigation and power works, roads, bridges, factories, townships, houses, offices, and so on. The job is done either departmentally, through the public works department, or through the award of contracts to other parties, domestic or foreign. In the former case, too, large purchases of various kinds of materials have to be made. For most of the purchases of materials and machines and awards of supply and construction contracts, the key sanctioning officials and ministers and their agents or go-betweens are paid an illicit and undeclared commission or bribes (also called kickbacks or cuts) by the suppliers and building contractors. The payments made are more than recovered by the suppliers and builders through various means, such as inflated cost estimates or supply prices approved by the officers concerned, poorer quality and shorter quantity of material supplied, substandard work, and false muster rolls for labour in departmental construction work. The government (and through it the public at large) are thus defrauded of public money, which could otherwise be used for public purposes. The result is cost escalation in government projects, poor quality of work executed and a perennial shortage of resources with the government.

Substantial portions of government allocated funds for various anti-poverty programmes, such as the Integrated Rural Development Programme (IRDP), never reach the designated beneficiaries. The truth is that, often, the expenditures shown in the books are not made fully in reality. Examples are expenditures on rural roads, dispensaries, schools, family planning centres, drinking water, and the maintenance of irrigation works. It is believed that ministers, politicians, government officials and other employees at various levels siphon off varying proportions of government allocated funds. In 1989, in a pre-election public speech, the then Prime Minister of India, Rajiv Gandhi, went to the extent of saying that as much as 85 per cent of the relief provided by the government for the poor is illegally charted away by intermediaries on the way, and only 15 per cent ultimately reaches the target groups. He further said that his party, if returned to power, would try to ensure that at least 30 per cent of government relief reached the designated beneficiaries!

The system of kickbacks or cuts also has become strongly entrenched in many government operations, so that the rate (or the percentages) of cuts in the value of supply or construction or consultancy contracts have become standardised. Foreign vending companies are said to pay up to 10 per cent of the value of the contract, and in the foreign currency of one's choice. The kickbacks on the Bofors gun deal with a Swedish firm and the HDW submarine deal with a German firm have been explosive political issues since 1986. The system of cuts has become further streamlined in that the distributive shares of government officials of various ranks and of the subordinate staff have also been standardised, and the cuts collected by a certain member of the staff are automatically distributed among others according to these standardised shares. This problem is not new. As it was noted more than twenty-five years ago by the Santhanam Committee (1964: 10), 'in all contracts of construction, purchases, sales and other regular business on behalf of the government, a regular percentage is paid by the parties to the transaction, and this is shared in agreed proportions among the various officials concerned.' The Committee was also informed by witnesses 'that in the constructions of the Public Works Department, 7 to 11 per cent was usually paid in this manner, and this was shared by persons of the rank of executive engineer and below down to the *mistry* (mason), and occasionally even the superintending engineer might have a share.'

Robert Wade (1982), in a unique study based on enquiries from several irrigation engineers and farmers, has estimated that, in the late 1970s, 25 per cent to 50 per cent of the annual works budget for canal maintenance in a south Indian state had leaked out as illicit income to engineers and others in the department. (Besides, these employees had extracted bribes from farmers for the timely and adequate supply of water.) All this had boosted their income several fold. Bribes for these postings were also paid to the transferring authority (the minister concerned). The National Institute of Public Finance and Policy (NIPFP) study (1985) has referred to two more studies on the subject. Pant (1979), in his study of the Kosi Canal system in Bihar, found that only 40 to 50 per cent of the recorded public expenditure was actually spent on works—the rest was misappropriated by the irrigation staff and the contractors. Talwar (1984) has estimated that 25 to 30 per cent of the recorded cost of public works in Delhi and neighbouring states was siphoned off illicitly by government functionaries, politicians and contractors, while it was as high as 80 per cent for land development and acquisition and 'minor works, maintenance and beautification works'.

Pilferage or Misappropriation of State Property: In several cases, pilferage of state property is said to be fairly significant. Common examples are coal at pitheads (for instance, through an organised mafia at the Dhanbad coal-mines in Bihar); foodgrains of the Food Corporation of India, both in transit and storage; cement and other construction material from PWD godowns and worksites; electricity, canal water, hospital supplies, wire and other materials in electricity and telephone undertakings, railway supplies, state roadways and so on. As a result of the regular pilferage of government stores, government expenditure on stores of all kinds goes up to make up for the losses and to meet the demands of its various ministries, departments and agencies. (To allow for losses due to pilferage, several government departments are said to have adopted the practice of overestimating their requirements of various stores.) Consequently, the cost of government operations, commercial as well as non-commercial, increases and its revenues from its commercial operations go down. Further, in most cases, pilferage takes place by and through the government employees themselves at various levels.

Bribes

Bribes as a form (or source) of black income is a very common phenomenon. They are mainly used to influence the decision of the authority dealing with a case, or the power to approve or recommend an application, or simply to forward a case file in a government office. Bribe-taking has spread to private-sector offices also, where bribes are paid even to get payment of bills duly passed. I have already referred to the practice of bribe-taking several times so far. My purpose here is only to explicitly acknowledge the wide occurrence of this practice and not to enumerate the main areas of their occurrence nor to proffer even a rough guess of the aggregate value of bribes given or taken each year. But, a casual observation of the consumption standards and accumulated asset holdings of the families of government employees that are given to accepting bribes suggests that this sum must be fairly large. Since bribes are mostly given and taken in a clandestine manner, they are not easily detectable, except in a few special cases. So, I shall not pursue the question of the aggregate size of bribe income any further.

However, two questions about income from bribes are worthy of our attention. One may ask whether bribes should be counted in any measure of black income, if we say that bribes only involve the redistribution of income between the briber and the bribed. We shall examine this question in the next chapter with respect to the view taken on the subject by the NIPFP (1985).

Another question worth examining is whether bribes are socially necessary or beneficial. At times, it is argued that bribes promote efficiency by cutting down delays and red tape, thereby saving the time, energy and effort of the management in procuring necessary official clearances and permissions (including licenses) and smoothening the flow of business activity. On the other hand, it is also argued that bribes breed corruption which, in high places, does not stop at small amounts, but extends to large kickbacks or cuts, running into several crore rupees. Besides, official delays and red tape at various official levels are time-honoured ways of extracting bribes from the public. The latter is made to pay if it wants to avoid delays, several trips to government offices and filing answers to all sorts of questions and queries. Further, in a regime of shortages, bribes simply help to jump the queue. They do not ensure that it is always the most deserving who gets the necessary official clearance or permission. The grantee of official favour may as well be the least deserving, though he may have spent lavishly to win official favours. Also, bribes may be the only practicable way out for crossing official hurdles for particular persons, but they are no remedy at the macro level.

The system of bribes imposes various kinds of social costs without any corresponding social benefit. Firstly, there are increased administrative costs due to overstaffing. The obstructionist and delaying tactics of the officials, induced by prospective bribes, greatly reduce the work efficiency and work ethic of the organisation. Since shirking work gets rewarded through bribes, employees have a built-in incentive to avoid and delay work. This is often interpreted as excess work in relation to a given workforce and the prevailing low norms of work. So, under pressure, the workforce gets expanded over time, without any improvement in work organisation and procedures. The result has been a continuous increase in the real resource costs of running the administration. Secondly, corruption at one place breeds corruption at other places through the demonstration effect. This greatly reduces the true effectiveness of govenment policies everywhere. Government measures, which appear sound and workable on paper, often turn out to be miserable failures when put into practice and other-than-target beneficiaries reap a major part of the intended gains. And all this is due to the system of corruption and bribery that has grown in the country.

5

Estimating Black Income

Introduction

Estimating black income is not an easy task. Most researchers have attributed this to the non-availability of reliable data. This is true, but does not encompass the whole problem. The problem is also partly conceptual and analytical, one of comprehending the vast scope and wide spread of black-income activities. In my view, the latter has been the chief shortcoming of the several attempts at estimating black income in India made so far. This should be clear from chapters 3 and 4 of this book. This point will be further illustrated in this chapter.

As a corollary, it also follows that the whole 'fiscal approach to estimating black income' (see NIPFP, 1985, Ch. 3), as has been used by Kaldor (1956), Wanchoo Committee (1971), Chopra (1982, 1985), and NIPFP (1985), is faulty, as it restricts itself to only personal income-tax evasion and the estimation of only personal income tax-evaded income. (The NIPFP had extended, somewhat, the scope of its estimation.) However, by common reckoning, this constitutes only a fraction of total black income. This will be discussed more fully as well as guesstimated at appropriate places in this chapter.

Before tackling the main point, some clarifications may be noted.

First, in my view, the measurement (or estimation) of black income should *not* be the main or primary task of economists or economic analysis. It would be better left to statistical organisations (such as the CSO in India). For economists, the appropriate task is that of analysis—analysis of the forces responsible for the generation and spread of black-income activities, their mutual interaction, and their various effects. Since black-income activities take on several manifestations and abound in diverse fields, it is equally important to study both the anatomy and the pathology of several kinds of black-income operations. Broadly speaking, these are the kinds of questions I have answered in this book. My discussion has not been inhibited by non-availability of firm global or sectoral measures of black income in India over time. What has been enough is the implicit assumption that the problem of black income exists in India, that it exists on a sufficiently large scale (relative to India's annual national income) to warrant our attention, and that the problem has been growing rather than decreasing over time. These assumptions are based on such diverse sources as casual empiricism and guesstimates, some special studies and government and newspaper reports.

Second, several attempts have been made from time to time in the past to estimate the amount of black income in India in a particular year. Starting with Kaldor (1956), other well-known examples in the field are the Wanchoo Committee (1971), Gupta and Gupta (1982), Chopra (1982, 1985), and NIPFP (1985). Some of these works, along with a few others, have been critically surveyed in NIPFP (Chs. 3 and 4) and Sandesara (1982, 1985). In my view, no useful purpose will be served (and some space lost) by going over this in detail. Yet we may note in passing that the key point of the Kaldor/Wanchoo Committee/Chopra method was the estimation of total assessable income, from national income accounts, on the basis of rough guesses about the proportion of non-salary income contributed to NDP at factor cost by each sector believed to have individual incomes, which are above the basic exemption limit for income tax. In comparison, the NIPFP report marks a distinct improvement (though it has its own short-comings) over the above method in estimating total assessable income. This will come out clearly in the subsequent discussion.

As a prelude to the problem of estimating black income in India, I shall take the NIPFP (1985) as my point of departure for various reasons. First, much organised research work by a group of scholars, supported by official agencies, has gone into the production of the draft of the NIPFP report, so that it has already come to acquire the status of a semi-official or quasi-official report, claiming much authenticity. Second, this report is the most recent document on the subject of black economy, and one of its estimates of black income (generally picked up by the media and the official agencies) relates to as recent a year as 1983–84. Third, a brief but critical evaluation of the report will illustrate very well several pitfalls in the estimation of black income and the unavoidability of guesstimating it from diverse sources, supplemented by much qualitative discussion on the multi-headed phenomenon of black income—an approach we have followed in this book.

The NIPFP Estimates of Black Income—A Critical Evaluation

The NIPFP report contains five different measures of black income—each one broader than the other. I shall sum them up below for analytical clarity, and for later reference and comment. The several measures are arranged in order of increasing value (coverage) of black income (generation).

1. BY_1: Non-corporate tax-evaded income, assuming the official NAS (National Accounts Statistics) data of the CSO (Central Statistical Organisation) are correct. This gives the narrowest measure of black income. It gives the amount of black income associated with gross personal income from current, legal economic activities and legal transfers (NIPFP, 1985, Ch. 5.1–5.7);
2. BY_2: BY_1 adjusted for possible underestimation of the official NAS data (NIPFP, 1985, Ch. 5.8);
3. BY_3: BY_2 + illegal transfers from public expenditures (NIPFP, 1985: 167, table V.9.1);
4. BY_4: 'Global' estimate of black income (NIPFP, 1985, Ch. 13) for the years 1975–76 and 1980–81 taking into account
   (*a*) under-declared sale values of immovable property,
   (*b*) leakages from public sector investment,
   (*c*) leakages from private corporate sector investment, and
   (*d*) black income generated through under-invoiced 'traditional' exports (NIPFP, 1985, table XIII.2.6);
5. BY_5: 'global' estimate of black income for the year 1983–84

(NIPFP, 1985, Ch. 13) = BY_4 + black income from illegal sale of import licenses and imported goods, and from smuggling of gold (NIPFP, 1985: 433, table XIII 2.7).

The derivation of the first three estimates of black income has been discussed extensively in Chapter 5, and of the last two estimates in Chapter 13 of the NIPFP report.

Several comments on the forementioned estimates are in order. They are discussed briefly below.

One, the first four different estimates of black income (BY_1–BY_4) are given for the two years 1975–76 and 1980–81. The BY_5 estimate is given for only the year 1983–84.

Two, whereas BY_1 is estimated in detail for the year 1975–76, that for the year 1980–81 is derived through extrapolation (see NIPFP, 1985, Ch. 5.7) with the help of a number of assumptions. The estimate of BY_4 used for 1983–84 (in the estimation of BY_5) is a crude extrapolation of the corresponding figure for 1980–81.

Three, each of the five estimates of black income contains some (small or large) element of guesstimate. The weight of this element of guesstimate increases as we go from BY_1 to BY_5. Whereas the NIPFP (1985: 168) admits the presence of guesstimation in the report, it has claimed that BY_1 is a 'genuine' estimate, as it is derived by 'detailed quantitative work' on objectively-collected primary data. In my view, this is an over-statement, because the exercise for even BY_1 does involve at least one step amounting to guesstimation. This is explained briefly in the next point.

Four, the main steps involved in the estimation of BY_1 by the NIPFP (claimed as genuine estimation procedure) are summed up briefly below.

(*a*) Two basic data sources are used to obtain a distribution of income by earners: the all-India survey of household incomes for 1975–76 by the National Council of Applied Economic Research (NCAER), which provides estimates of the distribution of income separately for urban and rural households (NCAER, 1980); and the official National Accounts Statistics (NAS) for an estimate of gross personal income accruing to households. Much ingenuity and some necessary assumptions have been made to convert the distributions by households into distributions by earners. Further, for analytical tractability, the actual distributions have been approximated by lognormal distributions.

(*b*) Since the total gross personal income estimated by the

NCAER survey falls subtantially below the corresponding estimate in the NAS, which is taken to be the 'governing total' in the estimation exercise—the former being Rs 45,100 crore in 1975–76 in comparison with the NAS estimate of gross personal income of Rs 64,500 crore, that is, the NCAER total being only 70 per cent of the NAS total, giving a shortfall of 30 per cent as compared to the latter—there was a serious problem of squaring the two sums. A part of the deficiency in the NCAER total was made good by adjusting the population data. But this reduced the divergence by only Rs 2,200 crore, and still left a large deficiency of Rs 17,200 crore (26.6 per cent of the NAS total) to reckon with.

(*c*) The aforesaid 'missing income' of Rs 17,200 crore was split in half between urban earners as a class and rural earners as a class (an important empirical assumption), though the unadjusted total income in the NCAER survey was found to be divided between urban India and rural India in the ratio of 1:2. The half-and-half division (in place of a 1:2 division) was selected on the assumption that the degree of under-reporting of income for tax was higher among urban earners than among rural earners. Further, in the interest of computation, it was assumed that, within the urban and rural categories, the proportion of under-reporting was invariant across income ranges, though it was admitted (at another place in the discussion) that under a progressive income tax structure 'the probability of under-reporting income to a household survey is likely to increase with income, in tandem with the probability to under-declare income to tax authorities' (NIPFP, 1985: 117). On the basis of these assumptions and treating the NAS total as the controlling one, the NCAER-based distributions were 'scaled-up'. It is worth emphasising that the aforesaid twin assumptions introduce an unknown degree of bias in the whole estimation. The size of guesstimate involved due to this bias cannot be gauged. However, its presence cannot be denied merely because it arises in the course of 'detailed quantitative work' and is not asserted as a single number.

(*d*) In the next step, using the 'scaled-up' earner-wise distributions of income, allowance is made for major exclusions, exemptions and deductions permitted under the Income Tax Act for different components of income (agricultural income, salary, business, and so on), and separately for the urban and rural distributions, to arrive at the estimate for 'total assessable income.'

(*e*) This estimate is compared with the total of non-corporate incomes actually assessed for tax to arrive at an estimate of BY_1, given by the excess of the former over the latter. The assessed income figures are published in the *All-India Income Tax Statistics* (AIITS). But, unfortunately, these figures, in general, are not based on the assessment year (except for a few years). For example, the published data for the assessment years 1976–77 and 1981–82—the years of special interest to the NIPFP for its research project—also suffer from this grievous deficiency of undercoverage. To make up for such undercoverage, the NIPFP uses certain 'blow-up factors' as approximations, given by the reciprocal of the ratio of the total number of assessments reported in the AIITS (on the assessment-year basis) to the number of assessees on the rolls of the department at the end of that year. But this is an extremely crude method of adjustment, because it takes into account only the number of assessees involved and not their net taxable income. It will give reliable results only if the average (net taxable) income of assessees in completed assessments equals the average net taxable income of assessees yet to be assessed.

Five, resuming our general evaluation of the NIPFP estimation of black income, it is interesting to compare its narrowest and so-called 'genuine' estimate given by BY_1 with the broadest 'global measure' (BY_4, which contains much guesstimation) for the years 1975–76 and 1980–81, reported in NIPFP, 1983, table 13.2.6. We find that, for 1975–76, BY_1 of Rs 3,471 crore (row 1) is a mere 31.5 per cent of BY_4 of Rs 11,870 crore (row 7) and that, for 1980–81, BY_1 of Rs 9,813 crore is only 41.4 per cent of BY_4 of Rs 23,678 crore. This shows that the relative weight of the guesstimated component in an estimate of BY_4 is much higher than that of the 'genuinely estimated' component. In other words, the BY_4 estimates are weighted heavily by guesstimation.

Six, at the next stage, the NIPFP (1983, Ch. 5.8) asks: What happens to BY_1 estimates if national income is underestimated? The answer leads to BY_2 estimates. To arrive at this answer, the NIPFP first reviews briefly the sources and methods of national income accounting used by the CSO in its Appendix 2. The object of the enquiry is to arrive at some qualitative judgements about the extent to which the 'value added' estimates for different sectors of the economy are distorted or underestimated by the practice of evasion of taxes and other economic regulations. The conclusions of the enquiry are noteworthy: 'that there is a strong *prima facie* case for suspecting a significant underestimation of total GDP . . . that such underestimation may be most pronounced in the following sectors: manufacturing (registered and unregistered), transport by any other means (than railways) and storage, trade, hotels and restaurants and other services' (NIPFP 1985: 162–63).

Regarding the extent of underestimation, the NIPFP tried out three different percentages of 5, 10 and 15 of GDP as its guesstimates due to evasion. (In most of its calculations, however, it had settled for 10 per cent). It was further supported by two assumptions: (*a*) that most, if not all, of the 'omitted GDP' accrued to earners who are already in taxable income brackets; and (*b*) that all legitimate deductions and exclusions have already been claimed so that no further ones are pertinent for the incomes associated with these omitted increments (NIPFP, 1985: 163–64).

These assumptions were made to obviate going through the process of estimation used for estimating BY_1 (point 4 of the foregoing). The implications of the above two assumptions were worked out numerically in two cases: (*a*) when three-quarters of the 'omitted GDP' was assumed to accrue to earners in the form of tax-evaded income, and (*b*) when this proportion was assumed to be half. The results are presented in a separate table (Table V. 8.1) for the years 1975–76 and 1980–81 for the aforesaid assumed proportions of three-quarter and half and the assumed percentages of 5,10 and 15 of the underestimation of official GDP and so its required 'inflation'. Thus, for each of the two years (1975–76 and 1980–81), six different estimates of additional tax-evaded income were obtained. (Obviously, the calculations can be repeated for different sets of values to the two percentages.) There is no fool-proof method of selecting a particular value for a particular year. (The NIPFP had shown a preference for middle values over chosen extreme values.) Some comments are in order here:

1. The range of guesstimates of 'additional' tax-evaded income to allow for underestimation of GDP is quite large. For example, for 1975–76, it varies from Rs 1,659 crore to Rs 7,467 crore, when the 'genuine' estimate of BY_1 was only Rs 3,741 crore. (Similarly for the year 1980–81).
2. If the official GDP is adjusted upwards by 10 per cent and three-quarter of this increment is assumed to take the form

of tax-evaded income, an associated 'additional' tax-evaded income of almost Rs 5,000 crore has to be added to the earlier maximum estimate of BY_1 of Rs 3,741 crore to arrive at the 'adjusted' estimate of tax-evaded income (represented by our symbol BY_2). As pointed out by the NIPFP (1985: 66) itself, this particular adjustment for evasion-related underestimation of GDP more than doubles its earlier highest estimate of tax-evaded income (BY_1).

Seven, the correctness or reliability of the NCAER household survey data was never examined or questioned by NIPFP, though the whole estimation exercise involving the derivation of earnerwise distribution of income was erected on these data. But the survey data themselves are known to suffer from several kinds of errors. The crucial ones in the present case are those that arise from evasion-related behaviour. This neglect might have introduced errors of unknown magnitude in the estimation of tax-evaded income.

Eight, the forementioned points, 6 and 7, suggest that the 'genuineness' of an estimate is not purely a function of the ingenuity or sophistication of the methods used or the 'detailed quantitative work,' but also of the quality or reliability of the raw data used, which may, in fact, be more importantly so.

Nine, the NIPFP's view (meaning and scope) of the phenomenon of 'black income' was faulty. It started out by equating it with (non-corporate) 'tax-evaded income'. This was in deference to the primary concern of the sponsors of the study—the Central Board of Direct Taxes (CBDT), (NIPFP, 1985: 15). More specifically, the concept of income chosen was only personal income, leaving out even taxable corporate profits. Personal income considered was only such income from current, legal economic activities and legal transfers. Thus, all incomes made illegally in myriad ways (such as through rampant bribes) listed illustratively in the NIPFP report (1985: 22–23) were ignored. This explains why the NAS total of gross personal income chosen by the NIPFP as the 'governing total' had to be adjusted upward for its underestimation. This underestimation was assumed to arise in respect of current, legal economic activities whose 'value added' was un- or under-reported to tax authorities. But this view unduly constricts the true scope of black income which, in actual life, consists of large amounts of transfer incomes (such as bribes, profits from black marketing, smuggling or the sale of import licenses or imported goods). That is why even the NIPFP is constrained to spread its net of black income estimation successively wider as it moves from one measure to another. But this is done very selectively, as is discussed under the next point. Here, the main point to note is that the concept of black income is fundamentally different from the concept of 'value added' used in the estimation of GDP or other national income measures. The only thing to keep in mind is that double counting of the same income must be avoided at all costs.

Ten, the coverage of the NIPFP's study of black-income generation is excessively narrow, as it totally ignores several important sources of black-income generation, such as tax-evasion of indirect taxes (excise duties, customs duties, sales tax) and corporation tax. Its defence of the neglect of the tax-evasion of some incomes (such as corporation profits and bribes) is untenable, as I shall argue separately under the next two points. Its provisions for some of the left-out sources of black income due to leakages from public sector investment and private sector corporate investment and through smuggling are highly inadequate. This applies to several other sources of black income as well. These inadequacies and omissions will become clear from a later discussion in this chapter.

Eleven, the NIPFP (1985: 169) has admitted that the omission of 'tax-evasion from corporate incomes' is the 'most glaring lacuna,' and an 'obvious shortcoming' of their work. But it has defended this limitation on palpably incorrect or questionable grounds. First, it has argued that we should assess evasion of a certain income (corporate income) only once and not twice—once in the hands of the corporations and then again as dividend income in the hands of equity holders. But this argument is not tenable because, if corporate profits are under-reported, not only is corporation tax evaded but also personal income tax on the under-reported amount. The second consequence (personal income-tax evasion) follows because the unaccounted corporate income is not distributed as dividend among the shareholders. Instead, the unaccounted corporate profits are misappropriated by those who wield effective control over the corporations. The black profits are used by them for such purposes as feathering one's own private nest at home and in foreign countries through the accumulation of foreign funds and assets, expansion and diversification of business, high and wasteful consumption expenditure and foreign travel, large political contributions and bribery, and so on.

The second argument advanced by the NIPFP (1985: 170–71) for neglecting the evasion of corporation tax may be summed up thus: to the extent 'falsification of corporate accounts' leads to an underestimation of GDP and so of gross personal income which, in turn, biases downward the estimates of tax-evaded income, this is hopefully made good when the official GDP is adjusted upward arbitrarily, while arriving at guesstimates of black income (see point 6 made earlier).

This argument is also not satisfactory because, at best, it makes up for the evasion of only personal income tax on unaccounted corporate profits, but not for the evasion of corporation tax on them. Further, the crude upward adjustment in the official measure of GDP is of the nature of catch-all adjustment, which is supposed to pick up the impact of all the sources of underestimation of the GDP which arise due to the evasion of taxes and controls (and also due to the undercoverage of potential taxpayers as well as due to the shortcomings of the CSO's estimation methods). Under the circumstances, it is anybody's guess as to how much of the underestimate of the GDP is attributable to an understatement of corporate income due to tax evasion and how much to other factors. Then, given the growing overall importance of the corporate sector and the immense economic and political power it exercises in India's political economy, the evasion of this tax deserves to be admitted and studied in its own right.

Twelve, the NIPFP (1985: 173) excludes 'illegal transfers in the form of bribes from one individual to another' in its estimation of black income, on the ground that such inter-individual bribes do not swell the total of gross personal incomes—that an income should be counted only once and not twice over. Explaining this further, it has argued that 'the exclusion of a bribe in the hands of a recipient may be justified on the ground that the income was already taxed (in principle) in the hands of the donor' (1985: 173).

There are at least two things wrong with this argument. Firstly, it is not clear what principle the NIPFP is talking about. Tax evasion is not a matter of principle, but of practice or fact. In most cases, the bribers bribe out of black or tax-evaded and not tax-paid income. In such cases mostly, the very purpose of bribing is to gain and protect tax-evaded income. Therefore, exclusion of bribes results in the total neglect of such incomes—exclusion in the hands of both the briber and the bribe-taker, a sort of 'double exclusion' of this income. Therefore, counting it in the hands of the bribe-recipient will not ordinarily result in the double counting of bribes (income). Secondly, bribes are a very important mechanism in the whole gamut of black-income operations and political-cum-bureaucratic corruption. Neglecting bribes on the basis of a false national income accounting argument artificially suppresses this very important category of black income.

In terms of national income accounting analysis, the pertinent question to ask should have been: what services do the bribe-takers render for which bribes are a reward, or what is the value added to social output by the bribe-takers? For individual briber, no doubt, there is a direct *quid pro quo*—he is rewarded with a certain government permission or facility. But, mostly, this is only a distributive gain. From the social point of view, there may not be any net addition to social value; on the contrary, there may be a net diminution of social value caused by the erection of various hurdles for temporary relaxation, of which the official-politician exacts a price from the briber. Thus viewed, bribes do not add to social value, but may detract from it. But, surely, this is a different kind of argument.

It is worth pointing out that the aforesaid exclusion of bribes from an estimate of black income goes against the spirit and content of Chapter 3 (entitled 'The Extent of Black Income in India: A Qualitative View') of the NIPFP, wherein 'the myriad ways in which illegal incomes are generated' are briefly listed (1985: 22–23). I shall reproduce them below with some exceptions, discussed separately soon after.

1. Grant of licenses and permits in return for bribes or political 'contributions'.
2. 'Speed money' to accelerate administrative procedures.
3. The 'sale' of jobs, postings or transfers in various public services.
4. Regular bribes to petty functionaries from different government departments (for instance, factory inspector, boiler inspector, health inspector, police, tax inspector for different taxes); the collections are invariably shared with higher officials of the department concerned.

5. 'Pugrees' (bribes) to circumvent rent control legislation.
6. Bribes to alter land use zoning or to 'regularise' unauthorised structures.
7. Bribes to obtain and maintain scarce public goods and services, such as electricity, telecommunications, irrigation water and railwagon allotments.
8. Bribes to obtain public contracts.
9. 'Contributions' to political authorities at various levels, ostensibly to finance elections and post-election manipulations.

Besides, three black operations have also been listed along with bribes: black marketing of price-controlled commodities; various kinds of frauds in banks and other financial institutions; and 'leakages' from various public expenditure programmes.

In terms of determinants and working mechanism, these activities deserve to be studied separately, and not be lumped together under one category of bribes to government officials and politicians. Also, there are many more forms of black income-generating activities (see Chapters 3 and 4 of this study) which are included in the above list as, presumably, it was not intended to be an exhaustive list.

Thirteen, the NIPFP neglects totally all incomes earned through illegal means or activities, such as black marketing, adulteration of food articles, production of spurious drugs, liquor, and so on, charging of *hafta* by policemen or protection money by local toughs, forcible lifting of coal from dumps by the coal mafia, forcibly cutting down trees for timber in government forests or poaching of animals. (We shall examine smuggling separately.) The list can be lengthened. But a few illustrative examples are enough.

All these activities result in private incomes. That is why they are undertaken by the persons engaged in them. But any one of them may or may not add to value, which alone is taken note of in national income accounting. Even if all the above-mentioned activities are socially unproductive and they generate only 'transfer incomes,' they do result in the redistribution of income and wealth in an economy. Therefore, from the distribution angle, incomes howsoever made, whether in legal or illegal ways, matter in actual life. For an analysis of black incomes, this reality of actual life cannot and should not be shut out, even though all of us may abhor such incomes. Further, all such incomes will be taxable, if they were declared, which is not done as we all know.

Main Sources of Black Income and Their Guesstimates

There are so many ways and sources of generating black income that it is very difficult to list all of them. So, I shall concentrate on only the most important. We have already discussed in reasonable detail several of them in Chapters 3 and 4 here. As a prelude to guesstimating the approximate nominal value of each of the listed sources, let me first state briefly each source for correct identification and coverage. I shall guesstimate black income from each of these sources for three selected years—1980–81, 1983–84 and 1987–88. The base data for guesstimation have been largely drawn from the CSO (*National Accounts Statistics*, 1990) and the RBI, *Report on Currency and Finance* (annual), various issues.

1. *Evasion of Personal Income Tax*: Maximum effort was devoted to an estimate of this kind of evasion in the report of the NIPFP. I have already discussed critically the main features of this exercise, along with its several shortcomings. I shall carry forward the percentage of 8.59 per cent of GDP, at factor cost, as the estimate of non-corporate tax-evaded income for 1980–81 made by the NIPFP (1985: 160, table v.7.2) on the tentative assumption that the NAS estimate of the GDP at factor cost is correct. For later years, retaining the above tentative assumption, we assume that the percentage of evasion had become progressively somewhat higher—9.2 in 1983–84 and 10.0 in 1987–88.

Based on the above assumptions, the revised estimates of GDP at factor cost (at current prices) in the NAS (1990, Statement 10) of Rs 122,206 crore, Rs 185,991 crore and Rs 294,408 crore in 1980–81, 1983–84 and 1987–88, respectively, puts black income through evasion of personal income tax at Rs 10,497 crore, Rs 17,111 crore and Rs 29,441 crore, respectively.

2. *Correction for Underestimate of GDP*: Following the NIPFP, I shall make an upward adjustment in the estimation of the non-corporate tax-evaded income made under 'Evasion of Personal Income Tax' above, because the GDP itself is said to be underestimated in the NAS. In my view, the NIPFP's adjustment is on the low side. I have already discussed (under point 6 earlier) alternative scenarios for adjusting percentages and values. All these are guesstimates and not genuine estimates. For reasons given in the foregoing, I have favoured higher guesses. So we shall assume that (*a*) the NAS underestimates GDP by 15 per cent, and that (*b*) 80 per cent of it accrues to income-tax payers. This guesstimate will straightaway add 12 per cent of GDP to tax-evaded income estimated under point (1) above. On applying this factor to the estimates of GDP at factor cost (current prices) given in the previous paragraph, we get the required upward adjustment of the black income figures given under point (1) above. These adjustments are Rs 14,665 crore, Rs 22,319 crore and Rs 34,329 crore for the three respective years.

3. *Evasion of Corporation Tax*: The evasion of corporation tax in India is quite common. This is done largely through the manipulation of company accounts, so as to reduce its net taxable profits as far as possible. This is over and above the evasion of excise duty and customs duty on imported goods. The NIPFP (1985: 424) had specifically mentioned black income generated from private corporate investment. Assuming it to be at a maximum of 15 per cent of investment, it had placed such black income for 1980–81 at Rs 325 crore, which was about 25 per cent of the corporation tax realisation of Rs 1,311 crore for that year. I shall count it separately under the section 'Black Income from Private Corporate Investment'. Since many *other* forms of tax evasion involving, say, overstatement of various items of expenditure and understatement of true incomes are resorted to, we guess the corporate tax evasion to be equal to at least 30 per cent of the corporation tax actually collected in a year. This gives us black income through corporation tax evasion of Rs 393 crore, Rs 743 crore and Rs 1,030 crore for the years 1980–81, 1983–84 and 1987–88, respectively.

4. *Black Gains in Urban Real Estate*: I have already discussed black operations (and black gains) in urban real estate. It is generally held that urban real estate, more so in the metropolitan cities of Bombay, Calcutta, Delhi and Madras, and other large and rapidly growing cities, such as Bangalore, is not only the most important form of holding black wealth but also a very important source of generating black capital gains. (Black income through tax evasion in the construction industry is supposed to be picked up under source 1 listed above.) Reliable data on the aforesaid capital gains are not available. The NIPFP (1985, Ch. 7 under the

authorship of Arun Kumar, and pp. 412–19) have made a heroic effort to produce estimates of such gains for 1975–76 and 1980–81. The method used consists of (*a*) ascertaining from official records and sample information of market sources the total registered value of immovable properties transferred in different states of India during a given year, and (*b*) applying to it a black-white ratio in which payment is made/received. On both counts, there are insurmountable difficulties, and we have to necessarily resort to guesstimates. Besides, as pointed out by the NIPFP (1985: 414), some transfers of immovable property do not require registration such as the shares of flats of Housing Cooperative Societies, or the value of property under the 'power of attorney' transfers. Further, the black-white ratio differs from place to place and has generally increased over time. For all these reasons, the NIPFP (1985: 414) assumed an average black-white ratio of 40:60 (or 2:3) for the whole country for the years 1975–76 and 1980–81. For the 1980s, the commonly-quoted black-white ratio in Delhi was 3:2. For our guesstimate, I have assumed the ratio of 1:1. (This will presumably make up for non-registration of 'power of attorney' transfers of immovable properties.) This will give a black-income estimate from the registered sale of real estate (excluding Delhi) for 1980–81 of Rs 5,254 crore (NIPFP, 1985, table XIII.2.1). Adding another Rs 46 crore for Delhi gives us a total figure of Rs 5,260 crore as the guesstimate of black income from this source.

Urban property values during the 1980s have grown very fast under the joint impact of general inflation, growing urbanisation and increasing scarcity of urban land. On the basis of casual empiricism, let us assume that the values of immovable properties, and with them black income, from this source have increased at the annual compound rate of 20 per cent. This gives us black income from this source of Rs 9,089 crore for 1983–84 and of Rs 18,847 crore for 1987–88. It should be noted that in the foregoing estimates of black-income generation, no account has been taken of other sources of black income generated in urban real estate discussed in Chapter 4.

5. *Excise Duty Evasion*: Various aspects of the evasion of excise duties have been discussed at length in Chapter 3. Since duty evasion is generally held to be widespread, and excise duties are the largest single source of revenue to the government, their total evasion amounts to large sums. In its main editorial, *The Times of*

India (New Delhi, 13 June, 1985) recalled that in 1973 the Excise Executive Officers' Association had estimated that 'leakages in excise revenue amount to at least half of the duty actually paid'. The editorial went on to surmise that 'it may well be much more,' given the vast increase in the purview of excisable industrial products and their producers and the rampant corruption in the excise department, which has presumably grown over time. I shall, therefore, assume that excise duty evasion for the period of the 1980s was at least 40 per cent of the 'potential duty amount' giving us two-thirds of the duty actually paid. On this assumption, the guesstimate of duty evasion yields the sums of Rs 4,333 crore, Rs 6,815 crore and Rs 10,951 crore for the years 1980–81, 1983–84 and 1987–88, respectively.

6. *Customs (Import) Duty Evasion*: I have already discussed the problem of customs (import) duty evasion. Such evasion is believed to be very high. In the absence of reliable estimates, let us assume that this kind of evasion was no less than 30 per cent of the customs duty due if there was no evasion. Based on this assumption, we can arrive at the guesstimate of evasion of import duties (gross) by multiplying the duty realised by 3÷7. As a result, we get figures of Rs 1,463 crore, Rs 2,424 crore and Rs 5,953 crore as our guesstimates for black income for the years 1980–81, 1983–84 and 1987–88, respectively.

7. *Black Income from Smuggling*: Smuggling is a 'growth industry' in India (see Chapter 4). Here, also, only guesstimates abound. Earlier, I had guesstimated the values of total smuggling in India in the years 1980–81, 1983–84 and 1987–88 at Rs 1,200 crore, Rs 7,000 crore and Rs 12,000 crore, respectively.

The NIPFP (1985: 432) had equated black income from smuggling gold with only its net profits (all of which remains unreported for income tax), and placed it at 25 per cent of its smuggled value. However, besides this, the major *direct* source of black income from smuggling is the evasion of customs duties and sales tax and black gains through associated *hawala* transactions. The average rate of customs duties in India has been more than 100 per cent *ad valorem*, and higher in general, on goods which tend to be smuggled (such as synthetic fabrics), apart from gold and narcotics whose import is totally prohibited. As a rough guess, let us assume that, overall, black income from smuggling is equal to the full value of smuggling.

8. *Black Income from Exports*: Black income from exports has been discussed in Chapter 3. In the three selected years of 1980–81, 1983–84 and 1987–88, our total exports were of the value of Rs 6,711 crore, Rs 9,771 crore and Rs 15,741 crore, respectively. Of these, about one-third were 'traditional' and the rest 'non-traditional'. Traditional exports are said to be grossly under-invoiced, whereas non-traditional exports are subject to both misinvoicing as well as malpractices and frauds of various kinds so as to gain maximum advantage from the export promotion schemes of the government. For the years in question, let us assume that the aforesaid malpractices in the field of exports might have generated black income at least at the rate of 15 per cent of the value of exports. This yields a guesstimate of Rs 1,007 crore for the year 1980–81, Rs 1,466 crore for 1983–84 and Rs 2,361 crore for 1987–88.

9. *Evasion of State Taxes*: The evasion of state taxes is a highly important phenomenon. Yet, this has not received as much attention from scholars and policy-makers as the evasion of personal income tax. An important recent study by Mehta (1990) carefully examines the evasion of three state taxes, namely, sales tax, state excise duty and entertainment tax in the state of Rajasthan. It was found that these three taxes, which had contributed around 73 per cent of the annual tax revenue of the state, had suffered from losses due to evasion of about 47 per cent of the estimated potential tax revenue in the year 1979–80. (Earlier studies on sales tax evasion for some states had come up with higher estimates due to defective methodology of estimation—see Mehta, 1990: 75–81). For present guesstimates of tax evasion of the aforesaid three major state taxes, let us assume evasion of 47 per cent of potential tax revenue from these taxes in all the states of India. The estimates are arrived at by multiplying the realised tax revenue by 47/53. Thus, for the three years 1980–81, 1983–84 and 1987–88, the realised tax revenues of Rs 4,967 crore, Rs 7,460 crore and Rs 14,114 crore, respectively, yield tax evasions of Rs 4,405 crore, Rs 6,615 crore and Rs 12,516 crore, respectively.

I have not dealt with evasion of other state taxes, which had yielded actual tax revenues of Rs 1,649 crore, Rs 2,302 crore and

Rs 4,833 crore for the aforesaid three years, respectively. Here, let us assume a modest 30 per cent rate of evasion of the potential revenue of these taxes, yielding the factor of 3/7 to be applied to the realised tax revenue to arrive at the guesstimate of the tax amount evaded. This gives us tax evasion of Rs 707 crore, Rs 987 crore and Rs 2,071 crore for the three years, respectively.

Adding the two figures of tax evasion for various state taxes, we get total tax evasion at the level of state taxes of the value of Rs 5,674 crore, Rs 8,447 crore and Rs 16,131 crore for the years 1980–81, 1983–84 and 1987–88, respectively.

10. *Black Income from Public Expenditure*: We have already discussed black income from public expenditure in Chapter 4.

The NIPFP has offered two different guesstimates for such black income for the same year (1980–81): one in Chapter 8 and the other in Chapter 13. The former takes the relevant subtotal of public expenditure as the sum of (*a*) public sector gross domestic capital formation (Rs 13,922 crore), and (*b*) net purchase of commodities and services by administrative departments and by departmental enterprises (Rs 7,913 crore). This gave the relevant subtotal of Rs 21,835 crore as the base for the guesstimation. The NIPFP tried three different rates of leakage (5 per cent, 10 per cent and 20 per cent) of this subtotal (1985: 266, table VIII. 4.1). In Chapter 13, it narrowed down its base drastically. It neglected totally 'net purchase of commodities and services by the government,' and under 'capital formation' considered only construction by administrative departments and by departmental *as well as* non-departmental enterprises (Rs 7,038 crore), and plant and machinery for Rs 325 crore by administrative departments only (1985: 421–22, table XIII. 2.3). This gave a smaller subtotal of only Rs 10,063 crore for the year 1980–81. The percentage rates of leakages assumed were also lowered.

The scope of the forementioned figures is rather limited, whereas the range of leakages from government expenditure is much wider. Such leakages are known to afflict various kinds of development expenditures of the government—more so of the state governments than of the Central government. So I shall guesstimate these leakages under two separate subheads: the states and the Centre.

The States: Let us assume that a minimum of 30 per cent of the development expenditure of states on revenue as well as capital accounts is siphoned off in one form or another. Such expenditure was of the value of Rs 13,644 crore, Rs 18,941 crore and Rs 38,599 crore in the years 1980–81, 1983–84 and 1987–88, respectively. (For each year, most of it was on revenue account.) Thirty per cent of these expenditure totals (amounting to Rs 4,093 crore, Rs 5,682 crore and Rs 11,580 crore, respectively) gives us the required guesstimates of leakage from state-level public expenditure and their contribution to black income for the year in question.

The Centre: In the case of the Central government, apart from its development expenditure (both revenue and capital accounts), defence expenditure is also prone to large leakages. The sum of these expenditures for the years 1980–81, 1983–84 and 1987–88 was Rs 9,304 crore, Rs 15,564 crore and Rs 24,751 crore, respectively. Here we assume 20 per cent of expenditure as the leakage rate. On this assumption, the guesstimates of black income from this head for the aforesaid three years come to Rs 1,861 crore, Rs 3,102 crore and Rs 4,950 crore, respectively.

11. *Black Income from Private Corporate Investment*: The necessary elements of guesstimation of this source have been spelt out in the NIPFP (1985: 424). According to the present guidelines, the promoters' contribution to the equity capital of a new venture must be at least 15 per cent of the total. It is widely believed that, most often, the promoters try to recoup this contribution in the initial stage of construction and installation of plant and machinery. This is achieved mainly through kickbacks from contractors and suppliers. Even if all promoters do not indulge in such practices to the same extent, this is said to be more than counterbalanced by family-controlled enterprises and closely-held small companies which tend to overstate investment expenditure to avoid payment of tax. For these reasons, a leakage of 15 per cent in relation to private corporate investment seems to be fully warranted. For the years 1980–81, 1983–84 and 1987–88, the latest estimates of gross fixed capital formation for the private corporate sector (CSO, 1990: 60, Statement 19) are Rs 3,541 crore, Rs 6,732 crore and Rs 11,942 crore, respectively. At a 15 per cent rate of leakage, black income from this source would amount to Rs 531 crore, Rs 1,010 crore and Rs 1,724 crore, respectively.

12. *Other Sources of Black Income for which No Guesstimates Have Been Made*: These sources are listed below. However, the list is not exhaustive.

1. Bribes, including illegal commissions, 'cuts' and kickbacks.
2. Black marketing in goods in short supply, such as steel, copper, coal, and other items of industry quota of raw materials and imports. There is also the black market sale of import licenses and foreign exchange (*hawala* transactions) at a premium.
3. Unaccounted interest earned from loans and deposits in unorganised credit markets.
4. Unaccounted stock-market profits on black transactions carried on in the private account of stockbrokers.
5. Income earned through the adulteration of food items, drugs, country liquor, production and sale of cheap imitations, forgeries and frauds of various kinds.
6. Leakages in public sector investments and in the working of public enterprises. At the state level, important examples are state electricity boards, whose combined losses over the Seventh plan Period (1985–90) had aggregated to about Rs 12,000 crore, some of which was surely due to leakages.

At the Central level, leakages are said to be common in several fields, such as coal-mining (the distribution of coal mined), purchase, storage and the transport of foodgrains by the Food Corporation of India, import and export of canalised items by the State Trading Corporation and the Minerals and Metals Trading Corporation (MMTC), railways and telecommunications.

The forementioned guesstimates are summarised in Table 5.1.

Concluding Remarks

Taking the estimate of black income of about Rs 51,000 crore for 1980–81 first, it may be legitimately asked: is this too much on the high side? It is hard to give a fully satisfactory answer when the question is posed in such aggregate terms. However, let us translate this question into micro terms of black income per household in the uppermost decile of the population in the distribution of income

Table 5.1
Summary Table of Black Income Guesstimates (in Rs Crore)

Source	*1980–81*	*1983–84*	*1987–88*
1. Income-tax evasion	10,497	17,111	29,441
2. Correction in (1) due to the upward adjustment of GDP	14,665	22,319	34,329
3. Corporation tax evasion	393	743	1,030
4. Black gains in urban real estate	5,260	9,089	18,847
5. Excise duty evasion	4,333	6,815	10,951
6. Customs duty evasion	1,463	2,424	5,953
7. Black income from smuggling	1,200	7,000	12,000
8. Black income from exports	1,007	1,466	2,361
9. Evasion from state taxes	5,674	8,447	16,131
10. Black income from public expenditures			
(*a*) States	4,093	5,682	11,580
(*b*) Central government	1,861	3,102	4,950
11. Black income from private corporate investment	531	1,010	1,724
12. Others	N.A.	N.A.	N.A.
13. **Total**	50,977	85,208	149,297
14. GDP at factor cost (current prices)	122,226	185,991	294,408
15. 13 as percentage of 14	41.71	45.81	50.71

and wealth. By common reckoning, this decile represents the rich and upper middle class in India—the class that has appropriated most of the black income gains year after year. The mid-year population estimate for 1980–81 was 690 million. That is, a decile of 69 million had 13.8 million families of five members each. This means that the average black income per family in this decile in 1980–81 amounted to about Rs 36,900 (or a little more than Rs 3,000 per month). It is much easier to comprehend this figure and also evaluate its likely correctness in terms of one's empirical judgement than to do so with the aggregate figure of Rs 51,000 crore.

We may apply a similar evaluation method to the aggregate black income estimate for another year (say, 1987–88) in relation to a similar estimate for 1980–81. For this, we convert our black income estimate of Rs 149,297 crore for 1987–88 at current prices into its value at 1980–81 prices. The NAS (1990) estimate of the

GDP implicit deflator for 1987–88 was 172.5, with 100 for 1980–81. Using this figure, the black income estimate for 1987–88 at 1980–81 prices is reduced to Rs 86,549 crore. Next, we note that the increased population of 800 million in 1987–88 would give us 16 million as the number of families in the uppermost decile. Using this number gives us Rs 54,093 as the estimate of average black income (at 1980–81) prices per family for the uppermost decile in the year 1987–88. Further, over the seven years of 1980–81 to 1987–88, GDP at factor cost (at 1980–81 prices) had grown by about 40 per cent. In comparison, over the same seven years, black income per family in the uppermost population decile, according to our guesstimates, had grown by 46.5 per cent. This yields an annual rate of growth of black income somewhat higher than the annual rate of growth of real GDP at factor cost. This would be generally acceptable.

6

The Consequences

Introduction

The consequences of black operations have been widespread as well as far-reaching—widespread because they have afflicted every aspect of our lives, political, economic and socio-cultural; and far-reaching because they have adversely affected the very foundations of honest social behaviour. The harm they have caused is not merely superficial but goes deep into the socio-political-economic structure. These effects need to be carefully comprehended and analysed, so that we understand more fully the kind of cancer that has been eating into the vitals of our system. I have already studied in detail the disease in all its dimensions. In this chapter, I shall review these dimensions and sum up the consequences under three separate heads—political, economic and social.

Political Consequences

Much damage was done to the honest and truly democratic functioning of the nascent political system by eroding political institutions, norms and processes before they had time to take root in the country. Healthy, democratic institutions are delicate plants which require careful planting and nurturing.

Political corruption flourishes in a system made up of persons with low moral values—those who have no scruples and with whom money-making (rather than public service) is the sole objective of their political activity and political being. With them, claims of performing public service are a facade—an instrument, an excuse—for staying in power.

It is only in such a climate that black operators in private business can be generally successful in bribing the authorities and criminals can enter and prosper in the political field. Such degradation of the office of politics keeps the honest and the upright away from it.

In Chapter 2, I have already discussed the subject of political corruption and the ultimate factors determining it. So we need not discuss this again.

Economic Consequences

Black operations have had several kinds of grave consequences for the economic system and the economy. The chief ones are discussed briefly below.

Income and Wealth Distribution: Under the impact of the continued generation of black income at a rising rate (relative to the rate of growth of measured national income in nominal or real terms), the inequalities in the distribution of income and wealth have grown over time and, more importantly, the concentration of wealth (and of control over the material means of production) in a few hands has also grown. And, to emphasise the point, a very large part of this concentration at the top of the distribution pyramid has occurred through the agency of large scale black-income generation. This, of course, does not mean that at other levels of the pyramid black-income generation is not important. For, at the medium and small levels of industry and trade also, black operations are equally rampant. In some quarters it is held that the ratio of tax evasion to the true taxable income of a small-scale unit, on an average, is much higher than it is in the case of larger units. Nevertheless, their individual proportion in the total annual black income or each one's absolute value is noticeably small, though this proposition need not be true for the small sector as a whole. For large businesses generally, however, both individually and collectively, the annual amounts as well as the shares of total black income are believed to be very high. In fact, it is widely held that each of the business empires has been erected largely on the strength of black income earned year after year and reinvested for business expansion and also used otherwise. This is not surprising in view of the several sources of black-income generation discussed in this book, and most of these sources being exploited simultaneously by the dominant firms.

All the forementioned descriptive propositions about the role of black operations and income in amassing large wealth or assets by large corporations, other firms and business houses are based on casual empiricism. Otherwise, the subject is such that it defies support from hard empirical evidence. (However, for the growth in concentration, see Goyal, 1979).

The forementioned trends in the concentration of wealth are also accompanied by a growing concentration of income in the uppermost decile. This decile largely comprises the business class, and such politicians and senior bureaucrats who have liberally used their positions of power in the government and administration for their own private gains. The old, traditional, salaried middle class, who were without much opportunity for extracting bribes from others no longer exists. Their place in the middle of the income and wealth profile has been taken up by burgeoning small industrialists and other businessmen (midddle-level traders), old professionals (lawyers, medical practitioners, engineers, and so on) and new professionals (chartered accountants and architects). The population at the bottom level has been growing incessantly, despite official claims about large declines in the percentage of people below the notional poverty line and the average rate of growth of real national income of about 5 per cent per year over the decade of the 1980s.

The forces working against poverty alleviation are many. The working of the black economy is one of them. It makes for an appropriation of a bulk of the gains from growth by the top decile of the income and wealth pyramid, followed by the new middle class, including a section of bribe-prone government officials and corrupt politicians.

Changes in the Economic Structure: The aforesaid developments have had far-reaching consequences in all spheres of our existence—economic, political, social and cultural. Economists, in general, do not take such a comprehensive view of black income, and the associated growth in inequality in the distribution of income and wealth and in the concentration of asset ownership and control. In the economic sphere, I wish to emphasise most the systemic or structural changes—the working of black operations in various spheres of the economy with active interlinkages with the political system has greatly strengthened the forces of degenerate private capitalism. This is the obvious, direct consequence of the growing concentration and centralisation of the material means of production, already referred to. This has come about in a big way through the proliferation of rent-yielding opportunities in the form of licenses, permits and quotas (see Krueger, 1974, and Appendix). Rent-earning by businessmen, and its sharing with the politician-bureaucracy complex, has created well-entrenched vested interests which have resisted the necessary reform of the system overtly as well as covertly. It is already well recognised in economic literature that the availability of 'rent-yielding' opportunities tends to encourage purely 'rent-seeking' activities, and the diversion of real resources from directly productive activities that they entail imposes a loss of welfare on the economy (see Krueger, 1974). In addition, the aforesaid phenomenon of rent associated with directly unproductive activities has promoted a highly debased form of capitalism—capitalism which is largely devoid of a spirit of enterprise, innovation, adventure, productive efficiency and fierce cost competitiveness. Such debased capitalism is partly also the result of the excessive and overdrawn protectionism and domination of the domestic scene by about a score of big business houses, controlled by as many families. At the lower levels, oligopolies and imperfect competition abound. Thus, to breathe competition into India's manufacturing industry and to make it cost and quality conscious in actual practice is the real challenge India's industrial economy faces today.

Impact on the Fiscal Economy: Black operations largely affect all aspects of the financial working of the state and its several apparatuses. They directly and adversely influence its revenue receipts—tax and non-tax—and indirectly its expenditure, borrowings from the public (including from banks and abroad) and deficit financing. We have already studied in Chapter 3 the problem of tax evasion, the various factors responsible for it (that is, the factors that encourage as well as facilitate it), and the several methods of tax evasion commonly practised. As a result, total evasion is very large (see Chapter 5).

Public expenditure is also adversely affected by black operations. In Chapter 4, I have already discussed leakages from public expenditure and the pilferage of government property. In recent years we have read much about kickbacks in the purchase of military and other hardware from foreign countries. These are only illustrative of 'corruption in high places' and represent, at most, the proverbial tip of the iceberg. The bulk of this iceberg of corruption lies under water, which the general public never sees in full. Presumably due to known or planned leakage, some projects are over-provided with funds initially. In some others, extra funds get provided through cost-overruns. In still others, the distant target groups for whom the programmes (such as Interated Rural Development Programme or IRDP) are drawn up are the main sufferers of the leakages on the way. The overall result of all these leakages is continued upward pressure on public expenditure to meet certain targets in real terms. 'Black leisure,' associated with general overstaffing in government offices, is also one kind of leakage from government expenditure. There are several other factors also which are responsible for the rapid growth of public expenditure in recent years, especially on revenue account. This is not the place to go into their details. For our purpose, it is sufficient to point out that illegal and manipulated leakages from public expenditure have been sizeable.

The net result of high tax evasion and large leakages from public expenditure has been large as well as growing 'fiscal deficit'. This deficit is met partly through borrowing from the public—in the form of both market loans and small savings—and from abroad, and partly through borrowing from the Reserve Bank of India, which involves currency expansion and its several effects. (The net Reserve Bank credit to the government is generally used as a measure of what is called the 'budgetary deficit' of the government.) I shall study these monetary effects separately under the next point. Here, I shall note only the effects of large and growing public debt on others—the domestic public and foreigners. First, as the interest cost of this debt grows, less is left in the budget for other heads of expenditure. This will not be a problem if the debt is used productively and the government regularly gets enough revenues from such investments to meet its rising interest bill.

Unfortunately, this has not been happening in the case of India. This is where the emergence of fiscal deficit on revenue account becomes specially worrisome. Loss-making productive uses will, of course, be relatively more troublesome for the government. But, in their case, there is at least the consolation of the coming up of potentially productive assets and perhaps the accrual of net social returns somewhere in the economy. External commercial debt, if large in relation to India's net foreign exchange earnings, can exacerbate balance-of-payment problems and also seriously compromise the country's economic independence. We may recall that all these consequences flow from the large and growing fiscal deficit occasioned by black operations operating on the revenue as well as the expenditure sides of the government budget.

Implications for Monetary and Credit Policies: Monetary policy is an important tool of aggregate demand management. So is credit control policy at the level of aggregate bank credit. At the aggregate level, monetary and bank credit policies are highly correlated, and so are affected in the same direction by various factors. In the sphere of credit, we have also to contend with non-bank credit, namely, term credit from development banks (such as the Industrial Development Bank of India), other financial institutions and the capital market (for corporate capital through equity shares and debentures), and the extremely heterogeneous sources of unorganised or informal credit (see Gupta, 1988). However, I shall mainly focus on only bank credit policy—aggregative and selective—and monetary policy.

Consider the monetary consequences of black operations first. They arise largely through 'excessive' budgetary deficits of the government. This may be explained briefly thus. We have already seen (under the previous point) that 'budgetary deficit' is that part of the fiscal deficit which is financed by net drawal upon the Reserve Bank credit to the government (through the sale of *ad hoc* treasury bills to the Bank), and that the large and growing fiscal deficit itself is traceable in a significant way to black operations. This budgetary deficit (or the net Reserve Bank credit) is the chief source of increase in high-powered money in India year after year (see Gupta, 1979) which, via the money-multiplier process, results in continuous increases in money supply. These annual increases have been on the excess side, in the sense that they exceed the absorptive capacity or demand for money of the public at stable prices and at full-capacity output. The excess increases of money supply have largely been inflationary in their impact. Thus, through a somewhat long-winded argument, black operations can be seen to be an important contributory factor for inflation. The resulting increase in prices serves both as an equilibrating process, and as an effect of this process which tries to bring about equilibrium between demand and supply in the money market. In other words, higher prices tend to raise the nominal demand for money, other things being the same. Alternatively, if we think of the demand for money in real terms, the rise in prices goes to reduce the real value of any quantity of money. To put it differently, any overhang of excess liquidity is a temporary phenomenon till such time as increase in prices has eroded it, or further excess increases in money supply have not restored it. In actual life, both the processes of erosion and restoration run side by side, though not at the same rate.

What do holdings of black money do to the effectiveness of monetary policy? It is hard to say, because we do not know much about the demand for money of the holders of black wealth who hold a part of their wealth in the form of black money. If it can be assumed that the holdings of black money also are behaviourally stable, responding to the same variables as the demand for 'white' money and with the same average intensity and confidence, then there is no identifiable reason for the effectiveness of monetary policy to undergo any systematic change. But, if they are relatively more responsive to the efforts and inducements of financial institutions (banks and others) and of deficit spenders seeking unaccounted loans, then there is a presumption that the aggregate demand for money of the public may have become relatively more responsive to changes in the rates of interest, and also less stable than otherwise. Other things being the same, this will tend to lower the effectiveness of monetary policy.

As an explanation of the foregoing, it may be added that black wealth is held only partly in the form of cash; another part is held in the form of fixed deposits with banks, foreign exchange (foreign bank accounts), units of the UTI, life insurance policies, gold and jewellery, real estate, and so on. Wherever possible, some of these assets may be held *benami* to evade easy detection. The placement of black money with private parties through informal credit markets is also believed to be quite large. These placements and other non-bank funds are not under the direct control of the RBI.

Nevertheless, the demand for black funds in the informal credit markets is affected by the availability and cost of 'white funds' in the market. For example, when credit stringency develops in the organised credit market (due to, for instance, policy measures), some of the unsatisfied demand for funds spills into the market for black funds and for informal credit. As a result, the cost and availability of black funds also tend to harden. We may call this the indirect effect of a restrictive monetary (credit) policy. The availability of black funds tends only to soften its rigors for deficit spenders, but does not render it nugatory.

These remarks apply equally to the selective credit control policy of the RBI. Such a policy is applied generally against an 'excessive' build-up of inventories of sensitive agricultural commodities, such as rice, wheat, cotton and oil seeds by large stockists, with the help of bank finance, in periods of their relative shortage and price rise. In discussions of such a policy, it is customary to point out that its success is partly frustrated by the availability of funds in the informal credit market, and the possible diversion of a part of bank credit for 'disallowed' inventory build-up, not on paper but in acutal practice, through the use of various subterfuges. The availability of black funds with the traders themselves (that is, owned by them) or through borrowing in the informal credit market only lends further strength to the aforesaid leakage to the selective credit control policy. This 'leakage' is not likely to be undone through the interest-rate effect, if bank credit is sought to be restricted only selectively and not generally, as the interest rates may stay unaffected.

Then, there are activities that are dependent largely or wholly for finance on black funds. Examples are smuggling, drug-trafficking, urban real estate, and the film industry.

We should also remember that all black 'money' is not passively held or even invested in income-earning financial and real assets. A significant part of it is also held actively, so that it participates fully in ordinary transactions at par with white money. The practical problem is that in meeting ordinary day-to-day bills for entertainment, travel, medical services, and so on, it cannot easily be said how much of the cost has been met out of black income and how much out of white income.

Black Income and Inflation: Black income is more a cause and less an effect of inflation. This is not easily discernible, because the black-income effect leading to inflation largely works indirectly and not directly. We have already seen how black operations lie at the root of fiscal deficit of the government, which is largely responsible for 'excessive' increases in high-powered money and so in money supply in India year after year. This is also the standard monetarist explanation for inflation, its continuance and acceleration over time. Fiscal deficit and associated inflation also necessitate the upward revision of administered prices after a lag, which gives a further push to ongoing inflation.

It is true that inflation tends to feed upon itself and, after a time, turn into a vicious spiral. But this does not happen all by itself; often, it requires the mediation of black-income activities. Since inflation is rarely fully balanced, its impact is highly disparate across sectors, some of which may suffer from pronounced scarcities. The result is black marketing and the reaping of windfall gains, which is not declared to the tax authorities. Soon this becomes a pervasive phenomenon, with increased hoarding and profiteering activities in sensitive commodities. The country's foreign trade also comes to be adversely affected by inflation, with the scarcity premia on import licenses and imported goods becoming quite high. Conditions deteriorate rapidly in a developing economy such as India's, which has been trying to develop quickly with the help of state intervention, planning, licensing and controls. In this climate of state-generated scarcities, greedy politicians with influence extract graft from people in business and industry, and government servants loaded with discretionary authority fall easy prey to bribes and blandishments. Thereby, corruption in the government and black-income generation in the economy spreads all round. The government's efforts to repress inflation through price and money wage controls only worsen the situation, as price controls encourage black marketing, and wage controls in the government further induce corruption and tax-evasion, and so on. Therefore, without cleansing the socio-political system, there is little chance for controlling inflation. In this redefined sense, current inflation in India is truly 'structural' or 'systemic'.

Distortions in Allocation: The allocative efficiency of a system is prized highly in traditional economic theory. Prospects of black income in certain activities, the need for the disposal of black income earned, and the placement of black wealth in relatively safe (with low probability of detection inviting legal action) and remunerative assets produces several kinds of distortions in the economy. Krueger (1974) has highlighted the welfare loss flowing from the use of resources in socially directly unproductive rent-seeking activities, such as the seeking of import licenses, and smuggling. Apart from the diversion of labour, managerial and entrepreneurial services from directly productive activities to these activities, they directly promote the creation of excess capacity in industry (in order to qualify for extra import licenses), deliberate administrative delays and hurdles in the grant of licenses, official clearances and permissions to extract bribes from concerned persons, and excess investment in education in the hope of landing bribe-prone government jobs (see Krueger, 1974; also see the Appendix in this book). With all this, we should, however, not forget the huge loss of potential output which the economy suffers year after year from unemployment and underemployment of labour and underutilisation of capacity, X-inefficiency (Leibenstein, 1966) or managerial inefficiency, and policy distortions induced by the corruption and greed of political decision-makers and administrators, coupled with the corruption and greed of decision-makers in the economic field. Any exhaustive list of distortions and deficiencies will be very long. The main distortions are discussed in this study at appropriate places.

Unreliability of Economic Data: Black income by its very nature defies correct measurement or even reliable estimation. Even then, rough estimates have been attempted from time to time (see Chapter 5). However, official data, which are widely used in empirical analysis as well as policy formulation and evaluation, continue to ignore it completely, treating it as if it does not exist in India—at least, that is clearly the message the official data convey to all concerned. But the truth is just the opposite. It is now universally acknowledged that the problem of black income not only exists but also that it has already attained vast proportions in relation to measured national income, and that this proportionate size is growing very fast—faster than the growth of measured national income. The faster rate of growth of black income is attributable to at least two factors—(*a*) the spread of black-income practices to more and more fields of economic activity, and (*b*) the rising share of black-income-prone sectors (industry, trade and government, and professional services) in the estimation of national income. The government has already been taking various kinds of policy measures to combat the evil of black income and black wealth, but without any success. In the field of data collection, estimation and their regular publication pertaining to black income, it must make an early and honest beginning. With all the resources, information and data-processing facilities at its command, the government is alone probably best suited for compiling the data on black income in the Indian economy.

The subject of gross errors in the measurement of economic data in India, arising from the total neglect of black-income phenomena, has been commented upon in the Wanchoo Committee Report (1971), Kabra (1982) and the NIPFP Report (1985). The main points are discussed briefly below. The discussion is not intended to be exhaustive.

First, all the official data about the state of the economy are highly unreliable, as they are not inclusive of any measure or estimate of black income. This applies to such crucial data as measures of national income, sectoral incomes, savings and investment, values of exports and imports or of foreign remittances into India, distribution of income and wealth, and the rate of growth of national income.

The gross underestimation of true national income and some sectoral incomes (such as of industry, trade and some other services) is a direct result of the neglect of black incomes. So nothing more need be said about them. I have also had several occasions to point out black income generation through various means in the fields of industry, trade (domestic as well as foreign) and government services. The accounts of trade flows are erroneous to an unknown degree mainly due to the under-invoicing and over-invoicing of exports and imports, and the smuggling in and out of goods. On capital accounts, too, a part of the remittances get leaked out to the black market for foreign exchange through *hawala* transactions.

Second, as a corollary of the foregoing, we should note that estimates of various key ratio variables (such as the capital-output ratio, the savings ratio, the tax ratio and income velocity of money), at the macro level are also undependable, because in each case either the numerator or the denominator (or both) of the ratio in question is (are) incorrectly measured, and the degree of proportionate error in them cannot be estimated. To take the simplest example first, consider the income velocity of money (V). Its value is given by the ratio of nominal income over the stock of money. Here, the denominator (stock of money) is usually measured without error, but the value of nominal income (the numerator) is measured with a large degree of error because it does not include any estimate of black income, which amounts to assuming its value being zero. This imparts a downward bias to the measured value of V. Also, if it is true to say that black income, as compared with the measured income, has been rising at a relatively higher rate, then the measured value of V has been suffering from an increasingly downward bias. Similar remarks of bias (in the upward direction) become due when we consider the estimates the tax ratio (i.e., of the ratio of total tax revenues of the government to national income). Here, the tax burden on the public is grossly overestimated or exaggerated because the denominator of the tax ratio is seriously underestimated.

Consider next the gross savings rate of the Indian economy given by the ratio of gross savings to GDP. The official revised data show that this ratio increased from a low of 14.0 per cent in 1967–68 to a high of 25.7 per cent in 1978–79. In 1987–88, it is estimated to have declined to 19.3 per cent. All these estimates of the savings rate presumably suffer from overestimation largely due to the underestimation of GDP, which is itself due to the neglect of black income. To the extent black savings (out of black income) are not captured in the official data and the measured savings are also underestimated, the aforesaid upward bias in the estimation of the savings rate is corrected. But it has been competently argued that, in actual practice, the underestimation of gross savings is not likely to be large (Raj Committee, RBI, 1982).

It is generally held that, *ceteris paribus*, black operations tend to make the distribution of income and wealth in an economy more unequal than before, because black incomes are relatively more unevenly distributed in favour of the already rich. However, this need not always show up in the recorded data, as is confirmed by the Indian experience. Here, the data on the distribution of income and consumption are compiled on the basis of household surveys. And we cannot expect such surveys to unearth true information about black incomes. Therefore, such data produced by these surveys are highly suspect.

The foregoing examples illustrate very well that, because of the presence of black income, the data on many key economic aggregates and ratios suffer from an indeterminate but significant degree of error. There are, no doubt, other sources of error, too. But, here, we are concerned only with errors due to black income which, as argued in the book, tend to have a systematic bias and predictable direction. This tends to vitiate any diagnosis of economic problems, policy formulation and planning, monitoring and the evaluation of policies. Thus, the derived damage is immense. The constant pressure and lobbying by the black operators complicate matters further for honest policy formulation and implementation.

Social Consequences

With continued changes in the economic basis of society due to ongoing economic development coupled with black income activity and the accumulation of black wealth, the social structure as well as social ethos in India have undergone substantial changes. Abstracting from caste and communal factors, the social structure is represented best by the society's class structure. Broadly speaking, black operations have greatly benefited the capitalists and the intermediate classes and harmed the working class. This is not to deny that several factors of growth and structural change with far-reaching economic and social effects have also been in operation in India over the past forty years or so. Important examples of such factors are the very large growth in industry and trade, the 'green revolution' in agriculture, making India self-sufficient in the production of foodgrains, and land reforms. But, as should be amply clear from our discussion in the book so far, practically all the processes of growth and structural reforms have been so worked that their benefits have been most unevenly distributed in favour of the already rich and powerful, namely, the capitalists, the large landowners and the intermediate classes (ICs) to the relative detriment of the working class. As a result, the capitalist class has become stronger over time, and there is increasing polarisation of the ICs towards this class. The mechanisms involved are a wide variety of black operations, including bribery and political corruption. In fact, one may go to the extent of saying that practically no business house engaged in industry or trade that has made progress in recent times has done so purely through honest means and the dint of enterprise, but has made ample use of black operations discussed in the foregoing in varying degree. Unfortunately, this is also more or less true of most flourishing professionals, senior state officials, politicians and others engaged in the service sector in high positions.

Regarding social ethos, as a result of the abundance of black operations, personal and social values of honesty, hard work, thrift and simplicity have been eroded and replaced by dishonesty, avoidance of hard work in government offices and most public sector undertakings and state-supported institutions (including universities and colleges), and conspicuous consumption and ostentation. The new generation of well-to-do people in cities has become increasingly fond of the five-star culture. Most of this development is due to large amounts of black income accruing to certain segments of the urban population, and a disproportionately large amount of black wealth accumulating in their hands. The demonstration effect of black income and wealth has worked very forcefully to entice more and more people into black income-earning activities and a luxurious style of living and consumption, bereft of any sense of social responsibility and commitment, and given to a vulgar display of riches and wasteful expenditure amidst a sea of poverty and penury. The associated fall in the social probity or morality of the people is the result and not the cause of 'corruption in high places'.

7

A Review of the Policies

In this chapter I shall review briefly the policy measures adopted by the government to deter income-tax evasion and unearth 'black money'. Similar measures in respect of other sources of black income are not being reviewed so as to save space and avoid repetition of the discussion of these sources in Chapters 3 and 4 in this book.

Measures to Deter Tax Evasion

The measures to deter tax evasion are summed up briefly below (for a fuller discussion, see NIPFP, 1985, Ch. 10).

Statutory Provisions: The statutory obligations of taxpayers have been presumably lightened. They include compulsory filing of tax returns by everyone with a taxable income, compulsory maintenance of accounts by businessmen and professionals and their compulsory auditing if income or turnover exceeds a specified limit, compulsory canalising of transactions involving payment exceeding Rs 10,000 through banks, tightening of the *benami* provisions of law whereby the *benamidar* has come to be recognised as the owner of the *benami* property in place of the real owner who had transferred this property *benami*, and so on.

However, in actual fact, these statutory provisions have not made much difference. The self-employed (such as, small businessmen and professionals) continue to escape the tax net either by not filing returns or by filing false returns with grossly under-reported incomes. However, the detection of concealed income in any year has been pitiably small.

Surveys: To bring new assessees into the tax net and strengthen the information base for the detection of tax evasion by existing assessees, a general survey is conducted by the income-tax department. This includes a door-to-door survey as well as information-gathering from outside agencies. While the surveys have increased substantially the number of taxable new assessees each year, the realised gain is much below the expected potential. The reasons for the relatively poor performance are said to be many. For example, the surveys are poorly planned, with little effective follow-up, corruption and inefficiency among the survey staff, their collusion with potential assessees, lack of proper supervision, and so on. Then, though the collection, dissemination and matching of information are highly crucial for income-tax investigation, these have been generally neglected. The information is either not called systematically or the information obtained is not properly utilised in assessments. Further, it is well accepted that information pertaining to income-tax evasion can often emerge from the enforcement of other taxes, such as excise, customs and sales tax, because most taxes are generally interconnected. But, in actual practice, the degree and quality of coordination among different investigation agencies under the Department of Revenue leave much to be desired.

Tax Raids and Seizures: Even the use of such drastic measures by the income-tax authorities has not been successful in rooting out concealed income and wealth. The reasons basically lie in the defective planning and execution of these measures and the excessive delay in the adoption of follow-up measures. Incriminating documents and unaccounted assets seized in raids are supposed to be utilised for prompt assessment and the swift imposition of penalty, followed by prosecution wherever called for. But, excessive delays in the processing of such cases allow the parties concerned enough time to invent explanations, and fabricate evidence. At times, information gets leaked out from the office of the tax authorities about impending income-tax raids, tipping off the targeted assessees, thus allowing the latter to dispose of incriminating evidence. Then, we have also to reckon with the widespread and growing corruption among the income-tax officials and staff, the escape route provided by the Settlement Commission (see below), and judicial protection.

The near-total ineffectiveness of the method of searches and seizures has made habitual tax-evaders bolder than before. In fact, it is said that some bold tax-evaders are so sure of their forms and methods of concealment of income and wealth or of providing an 'acceptable' explanation that they welcome income-tax raids, because infructuous raids will give them greater freedom from raids in the future so that they can indulge in greater tax-evasion than before.

Penalties and Prosecutions: To discourage tax evasion, tax laws also provide for monetary penalties and for the prosecution (and imprisonment) of tax-evaders. However, in actual practice, penalties have been imposed on only a very small proportion (less than one per cent) of total assessments and these, too, have been pitiably small. Even in such cases, the levy of monetary penalties can be appealed against, first to the departmental appellate officials and then to the Income Tax Appellate Tribunal, which is the highest fact-finding authority on penalty cases.

In appeals, the decks are heavily stacked in favour of the appellant owing to the provisions of the Indian Income Tax Act and their judicial interpretation by the Supreme Court. In particular, the Court has ruled that (*a*) since penalty proceedings are quasi-criminal in nature, the onus lies with the Income Tax Department to prove that the impugned amount is indeed the income of the assessee; and (*b*) the Department has to show that the income had been intentionally concealed by the assessee (the doctrine of 'mens rea,' which requires not just the proof of a fact but also of a state of mind or the intentions).

Further, the assessment proceedings have to be completed before the penalty proceedings can even be commenced. This places the tax authorities under a handicap, because while the Department has to support concealment on the basis of only the materials collected till the completion of the assessement, the assessee can rely upon evidence, fabricated or genuine, collected after the completion of the assessment proceedings. Also, the sequential nature of the entire legal process for arriving at a final decision on contested cases of penalties may result in a particular penalty case being drawn out for many years. Such a delay, in itself, further dilutes the deterrent effect of penalty provisions.

Besides these factors, there is the ubiquitous danger of bribery to the concerned officials, political pressure and inadequate and ill-trained staff for handling the rapidly growing number of penalty cases.

These observations apply equally to prosecutions for tax offences.

The Settlement Commission: Following the recommendation of the Wanchoo Committee (1971), the Settlement Commission was established in 1976. Its objective was to provide a mechanism for the quick and final disposal of those cases where a tax evader was willing to make a confession and face the consequences. To prevent the Settlement Commission from becoming a convenient escape route for detected tax-evaders, the Wanchoo Committee was explicitly against proceeding with the settlement of a case over the objection of the Income Tax Department, on the ground that concealment of income had either been established or was likely to be established. This was the position till early 1979, when the Finance Act, 1979 removed this crucial safeguard and left the Department with no veto power over applications for settlement. Now an assessee is allowed to apply for settlement at any stage and the Settlement Commission has wide powers to grant immunity from prosecution, not only under the Income Tax Act, but also under the Indian Penal Code and any other Central Act. On this, even the Supreme Court in one of its decisions has warned that 'secret understandings between high tax officials and big assessee businessmen are potential pollutants and convert Settlement Commissions into cover ups'.

Measures to Unearth Black Money

From time to time in the past, the government has unsuccessfully tried various measures, at least one of them repeatedly, to unearth accumulated amounts of black money in the economy. I shall discuss them briefly in this section.

Voluntary Disclosure Schemes: So far, five voluntary disclosure schemes (VDS) have been tried out—one in 1951, two in 1965, one in 1975 and another in 1985. Basically, these schemes had one thing in common: they tried to induce tax-evaders to declare their concealed income and wealth in return for taxation at concessional rates and immunity from penalties and prosecution.

Some special features of these schemes may be briefly noted. Of the two schemes of 1965, VDS I, also known as the 60:40 Scheme, had prescribed a flat rate tax of 60 per cent on all disclosed income. Since the total sum declared under the Scheme was only about Rs 30.8 crore, a modified version of the Scheme (VDS II) under the name 'Block Scheme' was later introduced during the same year (1965). Under this Scheme, instead of a flat rate of 60 per cent, different tax rates were made payable according to the blocks of concealed income disclosed. This Scheme was, therefore, much better received and the total voluntary disclosures amounted to Rs 146 crore. The Wanchoo Committee (1971: 12) had estimated that the total income disclosed in the first three schemes put together was a mere Rs 267 crore. The Committee had further observed that it was 'only a small fraction of even the most modest estimate of concealed income for the period of 15 years from 1951 to 1965,' and that 'as against this, the concealment detected by the Department in the ordinary course during a period of five years from 1965 to 1969 was Rs 161 crore and the taxes and penalties in respect of such concealed income worked out to Rs 105 crore, or about 65 per cent of the income detected'. The total tax yield of all the three schemes put together was a mere Rs 61 crore.

The VDS of 1975 was helped greatly by the fear psychosis generated by the Emergency. So, the total amount disclosed was of the order of Rs 1,578 crore—Rs 744 crore of black income and Rs 834 crore of black wealth. As a result, the government realised Rs 241 crore as income tax and Rs 8 crore as wealth tax.

The results of the VDS of 1985 have been equally disappointing. Commenting adversely on the Scheme and its outcome, the CAG (Comptroller and Auditor-General) has pointed out in his Report No.1 of 1990 that though the declarations under the Scheme involved 20.67 lakh assessments (with the total income and wealth disclosed aggregating Rs 10,778 crore), the gain to government revenue from the Scheme by way of collection of tax, interest, and so on, had amounted to only Rs 459 crore—a mere 3.87 per cent of the year's collection.

The voluntary disclosure schemes have been severely criticised by a number of reports of the Lok Sabha's Public Accounts Committee (PAC) (for instance, the 17th and 76th Reports of the Fourth Lok Sabha) and the Wanchoo Committee (1971). The Wanchoo Committee had stated categorically that they were 'strongly opposed to the idea of the introduction of any general ncheme of disclosure either now or in the future' (1971: 13). And yet two such schemes have been attempted afterwards—one in 1975 and the other in 1985.

The main points of criticism of the VDS (which are described well by the Wanchoo Committee) are summed up below:

1. Basically, they are schemes that permit converting black money into white on payment of a small amount of conscience money.
2. Disclosures made in the names of minors, ladies and *benamidars* have contributed to perpetuating evasion and rendered investigation in many cases of suspected tax evasion difficult or even futile. This is supported by the fact that, under the 'block scheme' of 1965, out of a total of more than 164,000 disclosures, more than 77,000 were from persons not previously assessed.
3. Much of the income 'disclosed' had already been 'detected' through surveys or searches and seizures. The 'disclosure' schemes served to protect the 'detected' cases from the deterrent provisions of penalties and prosecutions, thus undermining their effectiveness.
4. Such schemes place a premium on fraud and are unfair to honest tax-payers. As such, they weaken the level of voluntary compliance among the tax-paying public and the general morale of the tax administration. These effects are redoubled if such schemes are repeated every few years.
5. The view that such schemes help to rehabilitate the 'repentent' tax evader who is desirous of mending his ways is negated by the large number of 'repeated' beneficiaries who have taken advantage of all the disclosure schemes.
6. The Wanchoo Committee had also squarely rejected the argument that a disclosure scheme helps to broaden the base of investment and accelerate the rate of growth because, in most cases, the disclosed amounts are already invested surreptitiously in business or property through various devices.

7. Even at the cost of the abovesaid deleterious effects of the disclosure schemes, the revenue gains to the government from them, as seen earlier, have been highly disappointing in relation to even the lowest estimates of tax evasion.
8. Finally, the disclosure schemes, concerned as they were with past accretions of black money, did nothing to tackle the root causes of its generation.

Special Bearer Bonds (SBB) Scheme: In January 1981, through an ordinance, the government announced a new temporary scheme of SBB. Under this scheme, SBBs of Rs 10,000 each were issued at par with a maturity period of 10 years. The holders of these bonds would be paid Rs 12,000 per bond on maturity in 1991, thus implying an annual compound rate of interest of 1.8 per cent. The salient features of this scheme are as follows:

1. The bond holders have been given immunity from disclosing the source of money invested in SBBs and were not liable to any penalty or prosecution merely on the grounds of possessing such bonds.
2. Special bonds did not bear any names, that is, they were truly bearer bonds and thereby protected the anonymity of their holders.
3. The bond holders were given several tax concessions: the return at maturity was exempt from income tax and the value of the bond was exempt from wealth tax as well as gift tax. This was also designed to protect the anonymity of bond holders. Presumably for the same reason of anonymity, it was kept open to investors to bring the money received on the redemption of bonds in their books of account without attracting any tax liability.
4. Finally, the bonds were freely transferable and could be used as collateral security for bank advances.

Thus, the chief appeal of the SBBs lay in the anonymity, transferrability and immunity of these bonds and not in the rate of interest, which was very low by market standards. Yet, the market response to these bonds was not very enthusiastic, either because the black money operators did not have full faith in the assurances of the government summed up above, or because they did not carry that much extra cash and had invested well in business and property. So, though the initial sale of these bonds was closed on 30 April, 1981, it was reopened for another month in December 1981. The total subscription under the scheme was about Rs 875 crore.

The scheme of SBBs was widely criticised. It was called a bonanza for black money operators, a licence to convert black money hoards into white, or a device to confer ligitimacy to black money. It was also stressed that, like the voluntary disclosure scheme, the scheme of bearer bonds did nothing to check the fresh generation of black income.

In defence of the scheme, the then finance minister, Mr Venkataraman, put forward two arguments:

First, that, in effect, the bearer bonds imposed a 40 per cent tax on the buyer, because while Rs 6,000 invested in national savings (NS) certificates would yield Rs 12,000 in 10 years, it required an investment of Rs 10,000 in bearer bonds to yield the same sum.

The limitations of this argument were cogently described by Jha (1981). As stressed by him, the difference between NS certificates and bearer bonds is that the former must be bought out of post-tax incomes, while the latter is by definition bought out of pre-tax incomes. Anyone in the 66 per cent marginal tax bracket must, therefore, earn Rs 18,000 of pre-tax income today to earn Rs 12,000 in 10 years on NS certificates. Against this, he needs to earn and invest only Rs 10,000 in special bearer bonds. 'Thus, far from imposing a 40 per cent implicit tax on the buyer, the bearer bonds confer an 80 per cent windfall gain on him,' (Jha, 1981). In addition, they also free him from wealth tax, gift tax and death duty (abolised in 1985).

Second, that the real goal of the scheme of SBBs was to bring large sums of money out of the parallel economy to help finance high-priority investment through the budget. It was also claimed that this method of financing the budgetary gap was anti-inflationary, as it did not lead to any increase in money supply.

This argument was also criticised by Jha (1981) and Madan (1981), among others. The basic argument was that as the bearer bonds did not bear any name, they were highly negotiable assets; they were like high-denomination currency notes (demonetised in 1978) and were finding ready acceptance in lieu of cash as a medium of exchange in the parallel economy, as, unlike currency, these bonds were free from the risk of detection and seizure. Though the bonds would be encashable (with bonus of 20 per cent) only in 1991, they had been in circulation since 1981 and would have gained in premium over time. For example, according to a press report (*The Times of India*, 25 January 1985), Rs 10,000 bearer bond was being quoted at Rs 15,750–Rs 15,800 in Bombay, and bonds with a face value of Rs 1 crore were changing hands every day. Thus, depending on the velocity of circulation of these bonds, they must have been instrumental in 'financing' 'black money' transactions of the value of several times the amount of bonds sold by the government, and helping in the generation of more black income.

The monetary consequences of the forementioned developments can be interpreted in two ways. One is to follow Jha (1981) and Madan (1981) and say that the stock of money should be 'broadly' defined to include special bearer bonds, as they also serve as a widely-accepted media of exchange. Thus viewed, the sale of bonds does not reduce the stock of money: it only substitutes a new kind of 'money' for currency and hence, other things being the same, is not anti-inflationary. Futhermore, the sale proceeds from bonds are, at best, a temporary withdrawal of cash from the public. As the government spends it, the stock of cash with the public is restored. Therefore, on the whole, the scheme is inflationary, not anti-inflationary.

The other way is to look at the scene *via* the income-velocity of money. Under this approach, the use of bonds as the widely-accepted means of payment raises the transactions velocity as well as the income velocity of money. Therefore, even a given stock of narrowly-defined money will support a higher level of money income. This will indicate inflationary demand pressures, once the government has spent the sale proceeds of bearer bonds, other things being the same.

Demonetisation: The government has resorted to demonetising high-denomination currency on only two occasions, once in 1946 and again in 1978. (In 1978, the currency notes demonetised were of the face value of Rs 1,000, Rs 5,000 and Rs 10,000). Both the experiments were miserable failures. A rough index of the penal success of this measure is given by the value of high-denomination notes which were not presented for conversion. The usual assumption is that they were possibly not presented for fear of fiscal retribution. The actual outcome was as follows: in 1946, only about Rs 9 crore of high-denomination notes (out of a stock of Rs 144 crore in circulation) were presented for conversion; in 1978, the comparable amounts were Rs 20 crore and Rs 145 crore, respectively.

There are inherent weaknesses in any scheme of 'partial' demonetisation, for instance, the demonetisation of high-denomination currency notes only. (Full demonetisation, that is, complete replacement of old currency by new currency at a certain fixed rate of conversion, is highly disruptive of economic activity and so is generally avoided. Such currency reform has been adopted in countries which have suffered from a very high degree of hyper-inflation.) First, the high-denomination notes in India had constituted a very small part of the total amount of currency in circulation at any time. Second, currency (being non-interest bearing and easily detectable) is not an important form of asset for holding black wealth. Black-income operators generally hold only their transaction balances in the form of currency. Presumably not all of this is held in the form of high-denomination notes. Third, even for the holders of currency, there exist ways for converting high-denomination notes into lower-valued ones through intemediaries, though at a discount. Fourth, this method, too, does not address the basic causes of of black-income generation, the fundamental problem.

New Measures for Dealing with Black Money

Various new fiscal measures for dealing with black money were taken by the government during the year 1991–92. These will now be discussed.

Special Levy on Deposits in the National Housing Bank: Under the scheme, from the deposits made in this Bank by 31 January, 1992, a special levy of 40 per cent of such deposits was deducted to form the corpus of a fund in the Bank. This fund will be utilised to finance slum clearance and low-cost housing for the poor. The depositor has been allowed to withdraw the balance amount any time through account payee cheques. Persons making such deposits were not required to disclose the source of funds from which the deposits were made. The provisions of the Direct

Tax Laws would, however, apply to net deposits after deduction of the special levy. The levy itself is not an allowable deduction in the computation of income of the person concerned. The public response to the scheme was very poor.

Waiver of Penalty and Interest: The Income Tax Act contains a provision under which tax payers can avail of the facility of waiver of penalty and interest on the amount disclosed once in a lifetime. For those who have already availed of this facility, it was proposed to give just one more opportunity to disclose their unaccounted incomes through suitable amendments in the Income Tax Act.

Tax Deductions: To attract funds from the public for investment in low and middle-income group housing, highways, roads and bridges, non-conventional energy, school buildings and the supply of drinking water, it was proposed to provide for deduction, in computing the taxable income of a tax payer, the entire amount paid for financing projects or schemes promoting social and economic welfare.

Foreign Remittance Scheme: To attract larger inflows of foreign exchange to urgently meet the exceedingly difficult BoP situation, the government announced two special schemes on 24 July, 1991. Both the schemes were open till 31 January, 1992. Under the first scheme, remittances in foreign exchange could be made to any person in India. If the remittance was received as a gift by the donee in India, it was not subject to gift tax. The source of funds out of which the remittances were made was not subject to scrutiny under the Direct Tax Laws and Exchange Control Regulations. However, the provisons of Direct Tax Laws were to apply in the normal manner to rupee proceeds of these remittances. The scheme (over its duration of a little more than six months till the end of January 1992) led to an accumulation of foreign exchange to the tune of about $800 million.

India Development Bonds: Under the second scheme, the State Bank of India was asked to issue India Development Bonds denominated in US dollars. The bonds were available for purchase by non-resident Indians and their overseas corporate bodies. There was no ceiling for investment in these bonds, which have a maturity period of five years. The bonds are fully transferable among non-resident Indians. Interest from the bonds is exempt from income tax. The bond itself would also be exempt from wealth tax until maturity. For the non-resident holder, the face value of the bond and the interest thereon would be repatriable with exchange rate protection. The bonds can also be gifted to residents, who would be provided with amnesty and immunity on inward remittances. Such amnesty and immunity would be available only to the first resident donee. The gift would be exempt from gift tax. The resident donee bondholder would also be entitled to exchange rate protection and the same exemption from income tax and wealth tax, until maturity, but the proceeds would be paid only in rupees in India and would not be remittable abroad. Up to the end of January 1992 when the scheme came to a close, India had gained foreign exchange worth $1.6 billion through this device alone.

It should be noted that this scheme of NRI bonds denominated in US dollars to attract foreign exchange from NRIs and managed by the State Bank of India is nothing new. The previous two minority governments with practically similar features had tried it over the 3-month period—1 November, 1990 to 31 January, 1991. *The Times of India* (New Delhi) of 18 December, 1990 had called it the 'Black Money Whitener'. The paper had pointed out that specially transferable NRI bonds were being bought abroad and gifted to Indians in India. This meant that black money could be bleached by investing in these bonds. In fact, rupee hoards were reportedly smuggled out of the country and sold at a discount to purchase foreign currency in the Gulf to subscribe to the bonds. If the discount on rupees for the purchase of foreign currency was less, the bonds would have been more popular than they actually were and, consequently, the foreign exchange inflow from NRIs would have been larger. It was also said that the rupees going abroad would come back to India through unofficial channels, substituting for foreign exchange remittances from expatriates to their relatives in India.

Besides these, a couple of small measures to check income-tax evasion were also taken.

Gold Bond Scheme, 1992: In the Central government budget for 1992–93, besides the 'gold import scheme' already discussed, a 'gold bond scheme' was also proposed. The gold bond scheme aims at mobilising idle gold resources with citizens to supplement the official reserves. Under the scheme, citizens can obtain a gold bond in return for gold. The bond would be for a period of five to seven years, and would be liquidated by the return of gold or an equivalent value, at the option of the holder. It would enjoy a small income-tax free interest. The bonds would also be free of wealth tax and gift tax. As an added incentive, the holders of these bonds will not be asked any questions about the source of the gold holding—an important 'black-money-friendly' feature. It will also clean black into white. A new subsidiary of the Reserve Bank of India will manage this scheme, possibly from May 1992.

Concluding Remarks

The foregoing brief review of the measures adopted by the government to deter income-tax evasion and to unearth black money shows that these measures have not met with much success. This is fully corroborated by casual empiricism, which indicates that the evasion of taxes of all kinds and the generation of black income in the country have been growing over time (see also Chapter 5). Unearthing 'black money' through the issue of 'black money bonds,' with full amnesty as well as immunity from disclosure of the source of funds, is a clear capitulation of the government before the might of the holders of black money; officially it whitens holdings of black money in these bonds and emboldens hoarders to generate and accumulate more black money for their black transactions, under the firm conviction that the market- and black-income-friendly government will again be compelled by circumstances to offer them similar opportunities to whiten their black money. This is a highly damaging inference—damaging to the reputation of any honest government and to the hopes of the powerless masses who look up to the government to provide them with a clean government. In the end, we may say that the reasons for persistent policy failures to curb black income generation and unearth black money must be sought in the rampant political and bureaucratic corruption in the country—a hypothesis with which I had opened my discussion of black income in Chapter 2 of this book.

Appendix: Rent Theory of Black Income

What kind of theory of black income do we find in the corpus of economic theory? Nothing directly, as the very concept of black income has not been accorded any place in it. The closest approximation to a theory of black income is implied in the application of the concept of rent to various surpluses (over and above the opportunity cost of factors engaged or over the competitive rate of return of firms), which economic agents earn in situations of artificial scarcity created by government restrictions as, for example, through licenses, quotas or permits in various spheres of economic activity or through a wide variety of regulations and control. To give it a name, I have called such an implied theory the rent theory of black income in this Appendix. As an example, I would say that such a theory clearly underlies Krueger (1974), in her well-known paper entitled 'The Political Economy of the Rent-Seeking Society'. (The same impression is gathered from several other studies on rent-seeking.) The rest of the discussion in this Appendix is with particular reference to Krueger (1974).

First, only a small, but important, part of Krueger (1974) is concerned with the sources or forms of rent. To illustrate, she has provided point estimates of the value of rents for India (1964) in Table 1 of her paper (1974: 294). These estimates are reproduced in Table A.1

Further, Krueger has pointed out that the total value of rents (Rs 14.6 billion) was quite large in relation to India's national income of Rs 201 billion in 1964 (that is, equal to 7.3 per cent of the value of national income), and the problems India has faced trying to raise the savings rate.

She has explained briefly the meaning and basis of her estimate of each of the five sources of rent listed in the table (see Table A.1) in the form of short notes appended to the table. These notes are, however, too brief to throw much light on the nature and scope of each of the sources of rent. Krueger has also resorted to an arbitrary choice of figures for the values of rent-yielding activities and the rates of rent on them. Then, on her own admission, she has left out another important source of rent in the form of

Table A.1
Estimates of the Value of Rents: India, 1964

Sources of Rent	*Amount of Rent (Rs Million)*
Public investment	365
Imports	10,271
Controlled commodities	3,000
Credit rationing	407
Railways	602
Total	14,645

'industrial licenses,' because of the 'lack of any valid basis on which to estimate its value' (1974: 243). Therefore, her estimate of the total value of rents (not to speak of total black income) in India for 1964 is highly suspect.

We cannot afford to go into any detailed evaluation of the 'rent theory of black income'. Yet, its main shortcomings may be mentioned briefly.

First, this theory alone cannot do justice to an analysis of the complex of forces involved in the generation and appropriation of rents. Such an analysis will require unravelling of the nexus between the political and the economic, which alone can explain why government restrictions are imposed that generate rents, what determines the value of rents, and what mechanisms and forces intercede in the distribution of such rent-yielding opportunities among classes and individuals.

The funadmental problem of analysing the varied sources of black gains or incomes, their anatomy and pathology and their proliferation in an economy has not been given adequate attention. This is a very pertinent observation, as it implies that without knowing well the true nature of a particular kind or category of black income, there is no warrant for calling it rent. In other words, all black gains cannot be called rent. A few examples may be given here to illustrate the point. A small trader may suppress or understate his net taxable income and thereby evade personal income tax, apart from evading sales tax through the manipulation of accounts. He is considered to be engaged in legitimate trading activities, from which he may not be earning rent in a conventional economic sense, yet the undeclared part of his income (and the sales tax evaded) will constitute his black income. All bribes to public officials are black incomes, not rent. Some bribes may be paid only to expedite the perfectly legitimate and routine clearances and approvals. Leakages in PSUs may be simple pay-offs (from the suppliers of machinery, raw materials and intermediates, or from the contractors of construction works) to the public officials and the staff of the PSUs, or embezzlement and the outright theft of materials. (Similar pay-offs and embezzlement or theft may and do also occur in private businesses.) To call such payments and leakages rents earned by the employees of commercial enterprises is to overstretch the meaning of the term rent. And yet Krueger includes such leakages in her estimate of the total value of rents in India for the year 1964.

Second, the domain of the 'rent theory of black income' is highly restricted. In particular, it does not cover such sources of black income as tax evasion, drug-peddling, gambling, and smuggling.

Third, the 'rent theory' describes the source of all rent (and so black income) as government restrictions on the 'free working' of the market, implying that for the complete elimination of 'rents,' free markets are essential. But, as discussed at length in the main text, the sources of black income (and political corruption) are many and complex, such as gross inequality in the ownership of the means of production (material as well as human) and in the distribution of political power and influence. Also, a free market, too, may give birth to strong monopolies and oligopolies. It may also suffer from severe imperfections and uncertainties. Further, in an LDC, the economic role of the state without strong quantitative restrictions is generally regarded as necessary as well as socially desirable.

To be fair to Krueger, it must be stressed that her paper is not primarily an essay on the comprehensive 'rent theory of black income'. It only refers to scarcity rents created artificially by government intervention, and gives crude estimates of the value of rents in India (and Turkey) to make the point that the value of such rents was sizeable and that the availability of such rents tends to attract real resources into rent-yielding activities in pursuit of rent, that is, in rent-seeking. The main focus of Krueger's attention was to show that competitive rent seeking for import licenses (showing quantitative restrictions on imports) entails a welfare cost that is over and above the welfare cost of 'equivalent' tariff that would restrict imports to the same extent. (For a brief survey on rent-seeking, see Tollison, 1982.)

Before examining the rent-seeking model of Krueger, it will be useful to understand the content of social cost contained in rent and rent-seeking. It should be noted that in the literature on rent-seeking, an extremely narrow view of 'social costs' is taken—namely, that represented by real resource cost. In Krueger, the content of such a cost is illustrated by such items as the services and time of lobbyists and managers; the services of accountants and lawyers engaged in the manipulation of accounts for the realisation of rent; and the material cost on entertainment in hotels, air travel, and so on.

Bribes to officials are not specifically mentioned because they are treated as transfer payments. But, even then, they are a social cost as they lead to undeserved social inequalities, loss in work discipline and laxity in administration, and greater overall X-inefficiency.

Krueger (1974: 292–93) has also given some examples of licensing mechanisms which impose indirect real social costs on the economy in the form of installation of additional capacity even when it is expected to remain unutilised, lower-than-optimum size of firms in industries, and excess supply of persons seeking government jobs which carry high prospects for income through bribes. In all these cases, welfare loss is presumed to arise through allocational inefficiency of resources and not through enhanced social inequity.

We should note explicitly the following points. One, the distribution of rents or surplus (or black income) in an economy accentuates inequalities—in fact, a large part of the growing inequality and concentration of income and wealth in the society are largely a result of the phenomenon of rent and black income.

Two, the proliferation of rent as income and associated bribery engender widespread distortions in policy-making and implementation through lobbying and bribing, so that most policies are rendered infructuous in practice and the intended beneficiaries rarely get more than a small part (estimated at only about 15 per cent)* of the benefit budgeted (for example, under the various anti-poverty programmes of the government).

Three, the dominated classes are exploited and humiliated greatly by the members of the dominant class who have largely benefited from rents and other forms of black income and who, thereby, come to enjoy enormous social and political power, including power over the police.

Thus, the real resource cost of rent-seeking under economic analysis takes a very narrow view of the social cost entailed in rent-earning and rent-seeking.

I shall now examine briefly the main features of Krueger's model, which is designed to analyse the welfare cost of rent-seeking for import licenses. That the model is highly simplistic would be clear from its brief summary given below.

The Krueger model is a model of a small country with only a single factor of production (homogeneous labour) and only two productive activities: (*a*) agriculture producing food and (*b*) distribution, whereby food is purchased from the agricultural sector, and exported, and the proceeds are used to import consumption goods which are sold in the domestic market. Thus, only two goods (food and consumption) are consumed in the country under study. Food production is supposed to be subject to a diminishing marginal physical product of labour due to the fixity in the supply of land—another factor of production not explicitly admitted in the model. In the distribution activity, however, constant returns to scale are assumed to prevail, with a fixed labour coefficient of production.

* This is the percentage quoted by Rajiv Gandhi (then Prime Minister of India) himself in some election speeches for the November 1989 general elections.

Assuming perfectly free entry, Krueger (1974: 298) has argued that, if in the case of import restriction the wage in distribution exceeds the wage in agriculture (the only other competitive industry), '*people will seek distributive rents until the average wage in distribution and rent seeking equals the agricultural wage*' (emphasis added). With the 'distribution charge' per unit of import (p_D) and the permissible total quantity of imports ($\bar{M}$) policy-determined, the aforesaid condition of equilibrium will yield an average wage in agriculture (A') equal to $p_D \bar{M}/L_D + L_R$, where the numerator in the expression represents the total income of distributors, L_D is the quantity of labour engaged in distribution as defined above, and L_R is the quantity of labour engaged in rent-seeking. In her model Krueger assumes all distributors and rent-seekers as being partially engaged in each activity, though she admits to the possibility of the separate existence of pure rent-seekers also.

She further derives a very important proposition (1974: 300) which says that, in her model, the production cost of rent-seeking is equal to the value of the rents—that

$$R = A'.L_R,$$

where R = the total value of rents, and A' and L_R are as defined in the previous paragraph. It should be recalled that A' is the equilibrium wage rate of the economy.

Krueger says, further, that 'the value of rents reflects the value (at current prices) of the domestic factors of production, which could be extracted from the economy with no change in the final goods and services available for society's utilisation' (1974: 300–1). This much follows from the concept of rent. It is astonishing that Krueger attaches the same meaning to her crude empirical estimates of the value of rents in India and Turkey. This is so because she has jumped, without any qualification, from her highly crude and simple model of import licenses to the complex world of reality, for which even Krueger has recognised at least four other sources of rent (black gains). Moreover, the Krueger model does not fit even the Indian reality of the year 1964 (considered by Krueger), when import licenses are said to have commanded a premium of 100 per cent to 500 per cent of the import value of such licenses; even she had chosen (arbitrarily) a premium rate of 75 per cent. How does the equilibrium condition of the labour market in the Krueger model explained above square with these facts, and the implied rates of return on owned factors? Further, it is easy to say that rents are potential savings, and could be mobilised to raise the country's savings ratio. But, in practice, there are stupendous difficulties in the path of mopping up such rents (or black incomes). Again, the political factor and the socio-economic forces lying behind it stand in the way, and have to be taken into account.

As should be clear to the readers, Krueger's model of rent-seeking summarised above is far removed from reality. Its structural features and conceptualisation are not designed to capture the complexities and diversities of black operations or the allocation, subsequent resale and actual utilisation or even import licenses—the case chosen by Krueger as the most important source of black gains.

I shall illustrate these general remarks by evaluating the structural features of the Krueger model. All these features lead to the free entry of labour in distribution and rent-seeking. Three assumptions or structural features of the Krueger model are crucial for her particular results.

One, homogeneous labour as the only factor of production. This labour is equally relevant in agriculture and the activities of distribution and rent-seeking. In particular, it is implicitly assumed that no special qualifications, training and aptitude are required to enter the business of distribution and rent-seeking. More importantly, there is a complete neglect of capital and entrepreneurship—the other two key factors of production so important for most black operations, and even for Krueger's business of import licenses. Their total neglect is not innocuous for the working of the model and its results because their essential requirement can impose a constraint on complete free entry of resources into the business of distribution-cum-rent-seeking and hinder the attainment of equality of average wage (the proxy for factor returns) in agriculture and in distribution. Also, the requirement of capital (in a large enough amount) for business, coupled with sufficient enterprise goes to determine the initial conditions of firms and their prospects for bagging 'import licenses' and taking advantage of other government-created rent-earning opportunities. In today's world, most such rent-earning activities are highly capital-intensive, for which the initial ownership of a large enough amount of risk capital is a must. In a state where the distribution of this capital is highly skewed, entry into rent-yielding activities is generally restricted and not free. So the tendency to equate factor rewards across the board does not have free play. Specifically, the hired factors may or may not be allowed to earn small rents, but the owned factors of capital and enterprise may continue to reap rents without these rents being competed away and their average returns being equalised with the average rate of return elsewhere in the economy. Hence, we observe a highly skewed distribution of 'rents' in actual life.

Two, Krueger also assumes constant returns to scale in the rent-earning business of distribution. With labour as the only factor of production, market competition is supposed to attract it into distribution till the average wage rate in distribution reaches parity with the wage rate in agriculture. In actual life, economies of scale in industry and trade—the spheres of rent-earning and rent-seeking activity—are the order of the day. The operation of this factor also militates against free entry and free competition, and serves to protect rents and higher-than-average rates of return to owned factors.

Both these factors point strongly towards non-competitive rent-seeking.

Large firms enjoy another advantage over relatively small firms. In general, they enjoy much greater political clout and influence—an important source of the distribution of political patronage in various forms, including import licenses and other licenses, permits and quotas, and so on.

Three, Krueger also assumes risk neutrality. In all kinds of business (including agriculture), the risk of loss is ever present. In the pursuit of rents and of black gains, there is the further risk that rent-seeking may turn out to be unsuccessful (a total failure) and black operations, if successfully detected by the authorities, may land the black operator in trouble. Therefore, all business activities in general, and black operations in particular, contain a certain amount of risk premium in their incomes. Krueger's model has no place for risk and risk-takers. But the presence of risk in various kinds of activities and the differences in the degree of risk associated with them (even if not exactly measurable) as recognised by the business firms, including black operators, militates against the equality of pure (risk-premium-less) rates of return in apparently competitive economic activities.

For reasons discussed in the foregoing, we may conclude that the 'rent theory of black income' cannot serve as an empirically meaningful theory of black income.

References

Bagchi, A. 1974. 'Efficacy of Tax Incentives: "Tax Expenditure Analysis" and its Relevance for India.' *Economic and Political Weekly*, 15 June; 951–60.

Bhagwati, J.N. (ed). 1974. *Illegal Transactions in International Trade*. Amsterdam: North-Holland.

————. (ed). 1978. *Anatomy and Consequences of Exchange Control Regimes*. Cambridge, Mass: Ballinger (for NBER).

Bhagwati, J.N., and **P. Desai.** 1970. *India: Planning for Industrialisation*. London: Oxford University Press.

Bhagwati, J.N. and **T.N. Srinivasan**. 1975. *Foreign Trade Regimes and Economic Development*. New York: Columbia University Press.

Bidwai, P. 1982. 'Smuggling on the West Coast—I–IV.' New Delhi: *The Times of India*, 27–30 May.

————. 1983. 'Smuggling Assumes a Menacing Level.' New Delhi: *The Times of India*, 11 May.

Chawla, P. 1984. 'The Land Pirates.' *India Today*, 15 Feburary: 66–69.

————. 1985. 'Exchange Racket: The Money Changers.' *India Today*, 15 August: 124.

————. 1988. 'Smuggling: The Gold Rush.' *India Today*, 31 October; 102–5.

Chopra, O.P. 1982. 'Unaccounted Income: Some Estimates.' *Economic and Political Weekly*, 24 April: 739–44.

————. 1985. *Tax Ethics: Unaccounted Income or Black Income: The Norm of the Day*. New Delhi: Inter-India Publications.

Corporate Studies Group. 1981. *Functioning of the Industrial Licensing System* (mimeo). New Delhi: Indian Institute of Public Administration.

Dhar, R.N. 1990. 'Exports: Illegal Drain.' *India Today*, 15 May: 113.

Durkheim, E. 1970. *Suicide: A Study in Sociology*. London: Routledge and Kegan Paul.

Goyal, S.K. 1979. *Monopoly Capital and Public Policy*. New Delhi: Allied.

Gulati, I.S. 1973. 'HUF Tax Avoidance Revisited.' *Economic and Political Weekly*, 17 February: 397–402.

Gulati, I.S. and **K.S. Gulati**. 1962. *The Undivided Hindu Family: A Study of its Tax Privileges*. Bombay: Asia.

Gupta, A.P. 1984a. 'Tax Experience of Indo-American Joint Ventures.' *Economic and Political Weekly*, August: M-106–M-111.

————. 1984b. 'Management of Tax Expenditures in India.' *Economic and Political Weekly*, 24 November: M-122–M-132.

Gupta, P., and **S. Gupta.** 1982. 'Estimates of the Unreported Economy in India.' *Economic and Political Weekly*, 16 January: 69–75.

Gupta, S.B. 1979. *Monetary Planning for India*. New Delhi: Oxford University Press.

————. 1988. *Monetary Economics: Institutions, Theory and Policy* (2nd ed.). New Delhi: S. Chand and Company.

Hazari, R.K. 1966. *Structure of the Corporate Private Sector*. Bombay: Asia.

————. 1967. *Industrial Planning and Licensing Policy. Final Report*. New Delhi: Planning Commission.

Jain, L.C. 1983. 'Handlooms Face Liquidation: Powerlooms Mock at Yojana Bhavan.' *Economic and Political Weekly*, 27 August: 1517–26.

Jha, P.S. 1981. 'Bearer Bonds and Inflation: Mr. Venkataraman's Delusions.' New Delhi, *The Times of India*, 16 November.

Kabra, K.N. 1982. *The Black Economy in India: Problems and Policies*. Delhi: Chanakya Publications.

Kaldor, N. 1956. *Indian Tax Reform: Report of a Survey*. New Delhi: Ministry of Finance, Department of Economic Affairs.

Khadye, I.K. 1981. 'The Responsiveness of Tax Revenue to National Income in India, 1960–61 to 1978–79.' *RBI Occasional Papers*, Vol. 2 (1).

Kochanek, S.A. 1974. *Business and Politics in India*. Berkeley: University of California Press.

Krueger, A. 1974. 'The Political Economy of the Rent-Seeking Society.' *American Economic Review*, Vol. 64 (2); 291–303.

Kulkarni, G.B. (ed). 1984. *Price Controls in the Indian Economy*. Pune: Times Research Foundation.

Kumar, A. 1985. 'Evasion of Excise Duty on Sugar'. National Institute of Public Finance and Policy, Chapter 6.

Leibenstein, H. 1966. 'Allocative Efficiency versus X-efficiency.' *American Economic Review*, Vol. 66 (2): 392–415.

Madan, B.K. 1981. 'Black Bonds.' New Delhi: *The Times of India*, 31 December.

Malyarov, O.V. 1983. *The Role of the State in the Socio-Economic Structure of India*. New Delhi: Vikas.

Manor, J. 1983. 'Anomie in Indian Politics.' *Economic and Political Weekly*, Annual Number, May: 725–34.

Mansfield, C.Y. 1972. 'Elasticity and Buoyancy of a Tax System: A Method Applied to Paraguay.' *IMF Staff Papers*, Vol. 19(2).

Mehta, S. 1990. *Evasion of State Taxes in India*. New Delhi: Criterion Publications.

Mitra, S., and **R. Santhanam.** 1985. 'Narcotics: The Growing Threat.' *India Today*, 15 July: 126–28.

National Institute of Public Finance and Policy. 1985. *Some Aspects of the Black Economy in India*. Draft Report (mimeo). New Delhi.

Nayak, S.S. 1977. 'Illegal Transactions in External Trade and Payments in India.' *Economic and Political Weekly*, 10 December: 2051–62.

Ninan, T.N. 1985. 'Excise Duty Evasion on Cigarettes.' *India Today*, 31 October: 128–29.

Pant, Nandita. 1972. 'Leaking Foreign Exchange Tap.' *Economic and Political Weekly*, 22 June: 1407–14.

Pant, N. 1979. *Some Aspects of Irrigation Administration* (*A Case Study of Kosi Project*) (mimeo). Patna: ANS Institute of Social Studies.

Pick's Currency Yearbook. Detroit: Pick Publications.

Poulantzas, N. 1973. *Political Power and Social Classes*. London: New Left Books.

Prest, A.R. 1962. 'The Sensitivity of the Yield of Personal Income Tax in the United Kingdom.' *Economic Journal*, Vol. 72 (3): 576–96.

Rao, M.G., and G. Pradhan. 1985. 'Excise Duty Evasion on Cotton Textile Fabrics.' *Economic and Political Weekly*, 2 November: 1877–89.

Rao, V.G. 1979. *The Responsiveness of the Tax System in India*. New Delhi: Allied.

Reserve Bank of India. 1982. *Capital Formation and Saving in India, 1950–51 to 1979–80. Report of the Working Group on Savings* (Chairman: K.N. Raj).

————. *Report on Currency and Finance* (Annual).

Rishi, M., and J.K. Boyce. 1990. 'The Hidden Balance of Payments: Capital Flight and Trade Misinvoicing in India, 1971–86.' *Economic and Political Weekly*, 28 July: 1645–48.

Rudolph, L.I., and S.H. Rudolph. 1987. *In Pursuit of Lakshmi: The Political Economy of the Indian State*. Chicago: Chicago University Press.

Sandesara, J.C. 1982. 'Estimates of Unreported Economy in India.' *Economic and Political Weekly*, 20 March: 459–64.

————. 1985. 'Report on Black Money.' *Economic and Political Weekly*, 24 August: 1433–37.

Singh, A. 1989. 'New Route for Drug Smuggling.' New Delhi: *The Times of India*, 2 January.

Sinha, N. 1983. *Evasion of Excise Duty on Plastics* (mimeo). New Delhi: National Institute of Public Finance and Policy.

Srinivasan, T.N. 1973. 'Tax Evasion: A Model.' *Journal of Public Economics*, November.

Sundaram, K., and V. Pandit. 1979. 'Direct Tax Reform: Family as the Tax Entity and Other Reforms.' *Economic and Political Weekly*, 28 April: 776–81.

Sury, M.M. 1985. 'Buoyancy and Elasticity of Union Excise Revenue in India: 1950–51 to 1980–81.' New Delhi: *Margin*: 40–68.

Talwar, T.R. 1984. *Real Worth of Assets Created in Construction* (mimeo). Paper presented at the Conference of the Indian Association for Research on National Income and Wealth, December.

Tollison, R.D. 1982. 'Rent-Seeking: A Survey.' *Kyklos*, Vol. 35 (4): 575–602.

Wade, R. 1982. 'The System of Administration and Political Corruption: Canal Irrigation in South India.' *Journal of Development Studies*, Vol. 18 (3): 287–328.

Government Reports/Documents

Government of India, Ministry of Home Affairs. 1964. *Report of the Committee on the Prevention of Corruption* (Chairman: K. Santhanam).

————. 1965. *Report of the Monopolies Inquiry Commission* (Chairman: K.C. Dasgupta).

Government of India, Ministry of Finance. 1969. *Report of the Industrial Licensing Policy Inquiry Committee* (Chairman: S. Dutt).

————. 1971. *Direct Taxes Enquiry Committee. Final Report* (Chairman: K.N. Wanchoo).

Government of India, Ministry of Finance. 1971. *Report of the Study Team on Leakage of Foreign Exchange through Invoice Manipulation* (Chairman: M.G. Kaul).

———. 1973. *Report of the Central Excise (Self Removal Procedure) Review Committee* (Chairman: B. Venkatappiah).

———. 1978. *Report of the Indirect Taxation Enquiry Committee* (Chairman: L.K. Jha).

———. 1979. *Report of the Committee on Controls and Subsidies* (Chairman: V.L. Dagli).

———. 1980. *Report of the Expert Committee on Tax Measures to Promote Employment* (Chairman: V.M. Dandekar).

———. 1984. *Annual Report, 1983–84*.

———. 1985. *Report of the Technical Study Group on Central Excise Tariff* (Chairman: R.C. Misra).

Government of India, Ministry of Commerce. 1978. *Report of the Committee on Import-Export Policies and Procedures* (Chairman: P.C. Alexander).

———. 1985. *Report of the Committee on Trade Policies* (Chairman: Abid Hussain).

Central Statistical Organisation. 1990. *National Accounts Statistics, 1980–81 to 1987–88*.

Planning Commission. *Five Year Plans*.

Index